File
New...
Open...   Ctrl+F12
Close
Links...

Save   Shift+F12
Save As...   F12
Save Workbook...
Delete...

Print Preview
Page Setup...
Print...   Ctrl+Shift+F12
Print Report...

Exit   Alt+F4

Edit
Undo Clear Ctrl+Z
Repeat Clear

Cut   Ctrl+X
Copy   Ctrl+C
Paste   Ctrl+V
Clear...   Del
Paste Special...
Paste Link

Delete...
Insert...
Insert Object...

Fill Right   Ctrl+R
Fill Down   Ctrl+D

Formula
Paste Function...

Define Name...
Create Names...
Apply Names...

Note...

Goto...   F5
Find...   Shift+F5
Replace...
Select Special...
Show Active Cell

Outline...
Goal Seek...
Solver...
Scenario Manager...

Format
Number...
Alignment...
Font...
Border...
Patterns...
Cell Protection...

Style...
AutoFormat...

Row Height...
Column Width...

Justify

Bring to Front
Send to Back
Group
Object Properties...

Data
Form...

Find
Extract...
Delete
Set Database
Set Criteria
Set Extract

Sort...

Series...
Table...
Parse...
Consolidate...
Crosstab...

Options
Set Print Area
Set Print Titles...
Set Page Break

Display...
Toolbars...
Color Palette...

Protect Document...

Add-ins...
Calculation...
Workspace...

Spelling...

Group Edit...
Analysis Tools...

Macro
Run...
Record...

Start Recorder
Set Recorder
Relative Record
Assign to Object...
Resume

Window
New Window
Arrange...
Hide
Unhide...
View...

Split
Freeze Panes
Zoom...

√1 Sheet1

Help
Contents   F1
Search...
Product Support

Introducing Microsoft Excel
Learning Microsoft Excel

Lotus 1-2-3...
Multiplan Help...

About Microsoft Excel...

SYBEX **LEARN FAST!** BOOKS

The SYBEX *Learn Fast!* series offers busy, computer-literate people two books in one: a quick, hands-on tutorial guide to program essentials, and a comprehensive reference to commands and features.

The first half of each *Learn Fast!* book teaches the basic operations and underlying concepts of the topic software. These lessons feature trademark SYBEX characteristics: step-by-step procedures; thoughtful, well-chosen examples; an engaging writing style; valuable margin notes; and plenty of practical insights.

Once you've learned the basics, you're ready to start working on your own. That's where the second half of each *Learn Fast!* book comes in. This alphabetical reference offers concise instructions for using program commands, dialog boxes, and menu options. With dictionary-style organization and headings, this half of the book is designed to give you fast access to information.

SYBEX is very interested in your reactions to the *Learn Fast!* series. Your opinions and suggestions will help all of our readers, including yourself. Please send your comments to: SYBEX Editorial Department, 2021 Challenger Dr. Alameda, CA 94501.

LEARN Excel for Windows FAST!

LEARN *Excel for Windows*™ **FAST!**

Stephen L. Nelson

San Francisco : Paris : Düsseldorf : Soest

Acquisitions Editor: David Clark
Developmental Editor: James A. Compton
Editor: Alex Miloradovich
Project Editor: Janna Hecker Clark
Technical Editor: Martin L. Moore
Production Editor: Carolina L. Montilla
Word Processors: Ann Dunn, Susan Trybull
Book Designer: Claudia Smelser
Typesetter & Production Artist: Alissa Feinberg
Screen Graphics: Aldo Bermudez
Proofreader: Janet Boone
Indexer: Ted Laux
Cover Design: Ingalls + Associates
Cover Photographer: Mark Johann
Screen reproductions produced with Collage Plus.

Collage Plus is a trademark of Inner Media Inc.

SYBEX is a registered trademark of SYBEX Inc.

TRADEMARKS: SYBEX has attempted throughout this book to distinguish proprietary trademarks from descriptive terms by following the capitalization style used by the manufacturer.

SYBEX is not affiliated with any manufacturer.

Library of Congress Card Number: 92-80177
ISBN: 0-7821-1089-4

Manufactured in the United States of America
10 9 8 7 6 5 4 3 2 1

ACKNOWLEDGMENTS

A lot of people worked very hard so that this book provides you, the reader, with maximum value. I know it's difficult to connect with people you've never met and, perhaps, will never meet, but you should know that these people spent days and, in some cases, weeks of their time thinking about you and how to make one part of your life—learning and using Microsoft Excel—easier. So, who are these people? Well, here is the roll of honor for *Learn Excel for Windows Fast!*:

David Clark, acquisitions editor

James Compton, developmental editor

Alex Miloradovich, copy editor

Janna Clark, project editor

Martin L. Moore, technical editor

Carolina Montilla, production editor

Ann Dunn and Susan Trybull, word processors

Alissa Feinberg, artist and typesetter

Janet Boone, proofreader/production assistant

Many thanks to everyone listed above for a job well done.

Stephen L. Nelson

TABLE*of*CONTENTS

Introduction   xv

ONE Tutorial

1 *Getting Started with Worksheet Basics*   3

    Working with the Program   4
        Starting Excel   4
        The Application Window   5
        The Document Window   5
        Moving around Your Worksheet   5
        Finding Help When You Need It   6
    Creating Your First Worksheet   7
        Entering Labels   7
        Entering Values   8
        Entering Formulas   8
    Saving Your Work   10
    Exiting the Program   10
    Looking Ahead   11

2 *Building a Framework of Editing Skills*   13

    Retrieving Your Worksheet   14
        Understanding Worksheet Recalculation   14
        Undoing Mistakes   15
    Working with Ranges   15
        Erasing Ranges   16
        Copying, Cutting, and Pasting   17

Filling Ranges   18

Working with Cells, Rows, and Columns   19

    The Insert Command   19

    The Delete Command   20

Using Find and Replace   20

    The Find Command   20

    The Replace Command   21

Checking Your Spelling   21

Looking Ahead   22

3   *Enhancing Your Work with Formatting*   **25**

Using the AutoFormat Command   26

Working with Manual Formatting   27

    Aligning Labels and Values   27

    Assigning Formats to Numbers   28

    Changing Font Styles and Sizes   30

    Creating Borders and Shaded Cells   31

    Modifying Column and Row Size   32

Looking Ahead   33

4   *Printing and Managing Your Files*   **35**

Printing with Excel   36

    The Page Setup Command   36

    The Print Preview Command   38

    Options Menu Print Commands   39

Managing Your Files with Excel   41

    Handling Multiple Files   41

    Deleting Files   42

    Exporting and Importing   43

Looking Ahead   44

5   *Presenting Your Data with Charts*   **45**

Creating and Working with Charts   46

Using the ChartWizard   46

Working with the Chart Tool Bar   50

Saving, Retrieving, and Printing Your Charts   51

Saving Charts as Independent Files   51

Printing Charts as Separate Items   52

Looking Ahead   52

6   *Automating Your Work with Macros*   **53**

Recording and Running Macros   54

The Record Command   54

The Run Command   55

Macro Recorder Tips   56

Working with Macro Sheets   57

Looking Ahead   58

7   *Organizing Information with Databases*   **59**

Creating Databases   60

Defining Your Database   60

Entering Data   60

Working with Databases   62

Editing Database Records   62

Sorting Your Database   62

Finding and Extracting Records   63

Printing, Saving, and Retrieving   65

Looking Ahead   66

TWO   Reference

Add-ins Options   69

Aligning Values and Labels   69

Analysis Tools for Special Uses   70

Arranging Window Size and Position   71

Automatic Formatting   71

Bordering and Shading Cells and Ranges   73

Calculating Worksheets   75

Cell Protection   75

Charting Features   76

Clearing Unwanted Data   76

Closing Files   77

Color Palette for Document Windows   77

Column Width Changes   78

Consolidating Data   79

Copying Data to the Clipboard   79

Cutting Selected Worksheet Data   80

Deleting Columns and Rows   81

Deleting Database Records   81

Deleting Files   82

Displaying Document Windows   82

Drawing Features   83

Exiting Excel   85

Extracting Database Records   85

Filling Cell Data into Selected Ranges   87

Finding Cell Data   87

Finding Database Records   88

Font Styles   89

Form for Data Entry   90

Formatting Numbers   90

Freezing Panes on Split Document Windows   91

Goto Command   93

Grouping Graphic Objects   93

Grouping Worksheets and Macrosheets   94

Help for Lotus 1-2-3 Users   95

Help for Microsoft Multiplan Users   95

Help on Excel   95

Hiding Document Windows   97

Inserting Columns and Rows   99

Inserting Objects in Documents   99

Introducing Microsoft Excel   100

Justifying Text   101

Learning Microsoft Excel   103

Linking Files   103

Macro Recording and Running   105

    Macro Set Recorder   106

    Macro Start and Stop Recorder   106

    Macro Relative and Absolute Recording   106

    Macro Resume Recording   107

    Macros Assigned to Objects   107

Naming Ranges   109

    Applying Names   109

    Creating Names   110

    Pasting Names   111

New Files   112

New Windows   113

Notes on Cells   113

Object Movement to Back and Front   115

Object Property Control   115

Opening Files   116

Optimization Modeling   117

Outlining Worksheet Data   117

Page Breaks   119

Page Setup   119

Parsing Imported Text   120

Pasting Data from the Clipboard   120

Pasting Functions in Formulas   121

Pasting Link Formulas   121

Pasting Special Clipboard Data   122

Patterns and Cell Shading   123

Print Preview   123

Print Report   124

Printing   125

Product Support   126

Protecting Documents   126

Q+E Application   127

Repeating the Last Command   129

Replacing Cell Data   129

Row Height Changes   130

Saving Files   131

Saving Files in a Workbook   132

Selecting Special Cell Characteristics   132

Series Values   134

Setting Criteria for Database Search   134

Setting Database Ranges   134

Setting Extraction Ranges   135

Setting Print Areas   135

Setting Print Titles   136

Showing the Active Cell   136

Sorting Worksheet Data   137

Spell-Checking Documents   137

Splitting Windows into Panes   138

Styles for Worksheet Formatting   139

Table Command Scenarios   141

Target Value Modeling   141

Tool Bar Control   142

Undoing Mistakes   143

Unhiding Document Windows   143

Viewing Document Window Formats   145

What-If Modeling   147

Workspace Settings   148

Zooming in or out of Windows   149

Installation Instructions   **151**

Index   153

INTRODUCTION

I'm going to make this short and sweet. You didn't buy this book for my prose. You bought it to learn Microsoft Excel for Windows, in minutes rather than days or weeks. Before you get started, there are a few things you should know to help you get the most from this book.

HOW THIS BOOK WORKS

This book is divided into two distinct parts. The Tutorial section is a basic guide that shows you how to build and work with Excel for Windows worksheets, charts, macros, and databases fast! The Reference section not only supports you with detailed information as you work through the tutorial, but helps point you in the right direction as you gain skill with Excel's more powerful features.

Like the other SYBEX books in this series, *Learn Excel for Windows Fast!* employs clear, concise examples, valuable notes, tips, and warnings, and graphic features designed to enhance and speed your learning experience. An appendix guides you through the simple procedures for installing Excel.

TUTORIAL SECTION

The first part of this book is organized into seven lessons, each covering a basic spreadsheet topic.

Lesson 1: *Getting Started with Worksheet Basics* covers the basic knowledge you'll need to begin building Excel worksheets. It reviews the geography of Excel's application and document windows, and shows you how to build and save a simple Excel worksheet.

Lesson 2: *Building a Framework of Editing Skills* shows you how to retrieve a worksheet, undo mistakes, and use Excel's basic editing features. You'll learn to work with ranges, delete and insert rows and columns, find and replace worksheet data, and check your spelling.

Lesson 3: *Enhancing Your Work with Formatting* explains the tools Excel provides to make your worksheets easier to read and more visually attractive. In addition to the AutoFormat feature, topics such as aligning labels and values, formatting numbers, choosing font styles and sizes, and creating borders and shaded cells are covered in detail.

Lesson 4: *Printing and Managing Your Files* describes how to print your documents using Excel's Page Setup, Print Preview, and Options menu commands. You'll also learn how to erase unneeded files, export and import files to and from other applications, and handle multiple files in Excel's Windows environment.

Lesson 5: *Presenting Your Data with Charts* introduces Excel's chart-making capabilities. You'll learn to create, save, and print charts using Excel's ChartWizard feature and the special capabilities of the Chart tool bar.

Lesson 6: *Automating Your Work with Macros* provides some valuable tips and basic information on creating and running simple macros with Excel's Record and Run commands. This lesson also points the way to building powerful applications from scratch with Excel's macro sheet capabilities.

Lesson 7: *Organizing Information with Databases* teaches you to create, edit, and work with simple databases within Excel. You'll learn to sort, find, and extract records, and to print, save, and retrieve database files.

REFERENCE SECTION

Each alphabetical entry provides a brief explanation of the topic, the menu and command path, the shortcut key combination if available, and a description of how the command operation works. Cross-references and additional notes are also included when needed.

To make the Reference section more accessible, the title of each entry generally begins with the first word of the Excel command, or a common task description—such as inserting, deleting, cutting or pasting—that corresponds to the equivalent Excel task or command name. This method of titling and listing topics alphabetically should serve you well as you apply Excel to your own work and discover the power of the program through its system of menus and commands.

ABOUT MICROSOFT WINDOWS

This book was written assuming a basic level of knowledge and skill in using Microsoft Windows. Before continuing, make sure you know how to start and stop Windows' applications, choose commands from menus, and work with dialog boxes. These basics and this book are all you require to quickly learn how to use Excel for Windows.

PART ONE

TUTORIAL

GETTING STARTED
WITH
WORKSHEET BASICS

INTRODUCING

*Starting and working with
Excel*

Creating your first worksheet

*Saving your work and exiting
the program*

This lesson shows you how to start the program, work with Excel's windows, and create and save your first worksheet.

WORKING WITH THE PROGRAM

Before you begin, make sure Excel 4 has been properly installed on your system under Windows 3.0 or later. Start your computer, run Windows, and display the Program Manager window.

See Appendix A for detailed information on the installation process.

STARTING EXCEL

To start Excel from the Windows Program Manager, switch to the Excel program group window and double-click the Excel icon. You can also highlight the icon with the arrow keys and press ↵. When Excel has started your screen should look like Figure 1.1.

FIGURE 1.1:

The Excel application window with a blank worksheet

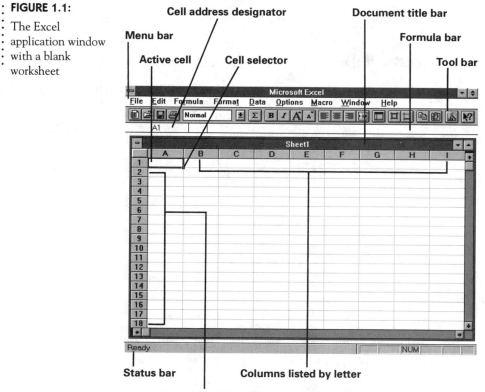

Cell address designator

Document title bar

Menu bar

Formula bar

Active cell

Cell selector

Tool bar

Status bar

Columns listed by letter

Rows listed by number

THE APPLICATION WINDOW

The Microsoft Excel title bar and menu bar are at the top of the application window. The tool bar, located just below the menu bar, is a series of buttons that allow for faster selection of frequently used menu commands.

The formula bar displays the data you enter into your worksheet. At the bottom of the application window, the status bar displays a variety of messages such as "Ready" to enter data.

THE DOCUMENT WINDOW

The document window is the area between the formula bar and the status bar. When you start Excel it automatically opens an empty worksheet file named Sheet1.XLS.

Under the title bar, the column border identifies each of the 256 columns in your worksheet with a letter of the alphabet. Excel uses double letters for columns 27 through 256.

The left edge of the document window identifies each row in your worksheet with a number. An Excel worksheet is 16,384 rows deep.

The intersection of a column and row is called a *cell*. Each cell has an address consisting of the column letter and row number. The cell in the top left corner of the worksheet is cell A1.

The active cell is identified by a dark outline called the *cell selector*. Figure 1.1 shows the cell selector in cell A1. The address of the active cell also appears on the left-hand side of the formula bar.

MOVING AROUND YOUR WORKSHEET

Since your worksheet is 256 columns by 16,384 rows, Excel provides four ways of moving and displaying it in the document window. Practice moving your worksheet using each of the following methods. Discover the techniques that work best for you.

With Scroll Bars If you've got a mouse, you can move your worksheet with the vertical and horizontal scroll bars that appear along the right and bottom edges of the document window.

Scroll bars are a basic element of the Windows interface. For more information on how to use them, refer to the Microsoft Windows User Guide.

With Navigation Keys The standard navigation keys, PageUp and PageDn, move your worksheet up and down a screen at a time. When you hold down the Ctrl key and then press PageUp or PageDn, your worksheet moves right or left a screen at a time.

Using the Cell Selector Excel moves the worksheet as you move the cell selector. You can move the cell selector in all directions with the arrow keys, to the right with the Tab key, and to the left by holding Shift while you press the Tab key.

Using the Goto Command The Goto command lets you move the cell selector to a designated cell address. Choose the Goto command from the Formula menu or press F5 to display the Goto dialog box shown in Figure 1.2. Enter the cell address in the Reference text box and select OK.

FIGURE 1.2:

The Goto dialog box

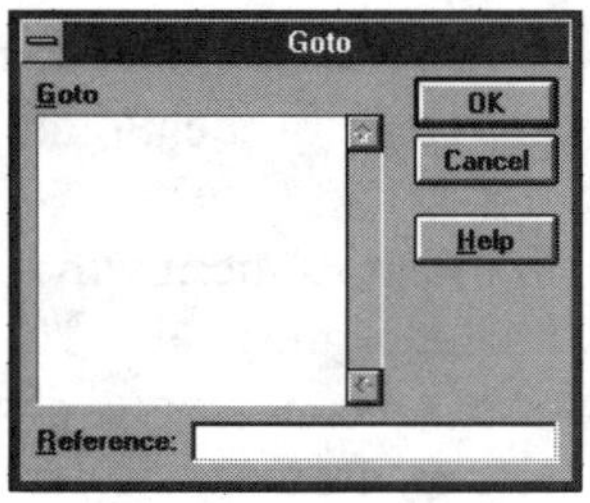

If you're working with named cells or ranges, their names appear in the Goto list box. You can move the cell selector to a named cell or range by choosing it from the list and selecting OK.

FINDING HELP WHEN YOU NEED IT

Excel uses the standard Windows Help application. To start Help, choose the Contents command from the Help menu or select the Help command button on the tool bar.

For help with Help, refer to your Excel documentation and your Microsoft Windows User Guide.

CREATING YOUR FIRST WORKSHEET

Excel lets you enter labels, values, and formulas in the cells of your worksheet. Let's construct a simple budgeting worksheet.

ENTERING LABELS

Labels are simply things you don't want to arithmetically manipulate. To enter each of the labels shown in Figure 1.3, position the cell selector by clicking your mouse on the appropriate cell or by using the arrow keys, and then type the label in the active cell. Excel displays the active label on the formula bar, and adds the Enter command button, labeled with a check mark, and the Cancel command button, labeled with an X.

FIGURE 1.3:

Your first worksheet with labels entered

			Microsoft Excel					
File	**Edit**	**Formula**	**Format**	**Data**	**Options**	**Macro**	**Window**	**Help**

A1   Advertising

	A	B	C	D	E	F	G	H	I
1	Advertising								
2	Bank charges								
3	Car & truck								
4	Depreciation								
5	Equipment rental								
6	Freight								
7									
8									
9									
10									

To complete each entry, select the Enter command button, press ↵, or move the cell selector. Excel aligns your labels to the left in each cell, and allows long labels to spill over into adjacent cells if they are unoccupied.

TIP

If you make any typing mistakes while entering your data, use the Backspace key to erase characters to the left of the insertion point and then retype the correct data. You can also reposition the insertion point with the arrow keys and erase characters to the right with the Delete key. If you don't want to enter the data shown on the formula bar into the active cell, select the Cancel command button or press Esc.

ENTERING VALUES

Values are numbers you want to add, subtract, multiply, divide, and use in formulas and functions. Figure 1.4 shows the values, or amounts, entered opposite each of your worksheet labels.

FIGURE 1.4:

Your worksheet with labels and values entered

	A	B	C	D	E	F	G	H	I
1	Advertising		500						
2	Bank charges		12.5						
3	Car & truck		100						
4	Depreciation		250						
5	Equipment rental		125						
6	Freight		75						
7									
8									
9									
10									

To enter each of the values shown in Figure 1.4, position the cell selector, type the value, and then select the Enter command button, press ↵, or move the cell selector. Excel displays values aligned with the right cell border.

To enter a negative value, precede it with a hyphen, as in −2. If a value is too large to fit a single cell, Excel displays it in scientific notation. The number 123456789 is displayed as 1.23E+08 and .0000001 is displayed as 1E-07. Excel doesn't display characters such as dollar signs, percent symbols, or commas when you enter them in a cell, but uses them to format those values. Excel also has a variety of date and time formatting options. Refer to Lesson 3 for more information on formatting.

ENTERING FORMULAS

The power of Excel is its ability to calculate *formulas*, in which you can use a cell's address to represent the value it holds at any given time. To add the budgeted amounts on your worksheet, move the cell selector to C8 and type =C1+C2+C3+C4+C5+C6. (You could have gotten the same result by entering =500+12.5+100+250+125+75, but then you would need to rewrite the formula each time any of the values changed.)

Typing an equal (=) sign tells Excel that what follows is your formula. When you press ↵, Excel calculates the formula and displays the result shown in Figure 1.5.

WARNING

It's possible to build illogical or unsolvable formulas or to create circular reference errors where two or more formulas indirectly depend on one another to achieve a result. Excel identifies circular references by displaying the word "Circ" on the status bar and showing the address of the problem cell.

Paste – for list of Excel functions

- **FIGURE 1.5:**
- Your worksheet with
- formula entered and
- displayed result

	Microsoft Excel
File Edit Formula Format Data Options Macro Window Help	

C8   =C1+C2+C3+C4+C5+C6

Sheet1

	A	B	C	D	E	F	G	H	I
1	Advertising		500						
2	Bank charges		12.5						
3	Car & truck		100						
4	Depreciation		250						
5	Equipment rental		125						
6	Freight		75						
7									
8			1062.5						
9									
10									

You can construct formulas that add, subtract, multiply, divide, and exponentiate. The – symbol means subtraction, the * symbol multiplication, the / symbol division, and the ^ symbol exponential operations. To raise 12 to the second power, use the formula =12^2.

Excel follows standard rules of operator precedence. Exponential operations are performed first, multiplication and division next, and addition and subtraction last. To override these rules, use parenthesis marks. Excel first performs the function most deeply nested in parentheses. The formula =((1+2)*3)^4 adds 1 and 2, then multiplies 3 by 3, and finally raises 9 to the 4th power to equal 6561.

TIP

Excel provides more than 300 standard formulas called functions that can provide a shortcut to constructing complicated or lengthy formulas. Rather than adding your budgeted amounts by entering the formula =C1+C2+C3+C4+C5+C6, you can use the function formula =SUM(C1:C6). Each function has a brief, descriptive name such as SUM or AVERAGE. A colon (:) can be used to indicate a running string of cell addresses. To display a list of Excel functions, choose the Paste Function command from the Formula menu.

SAVING YOUR WORK

When you first save a worksheet, you must give it a name and tell Excel where to store it. Let's save your worksheet using the File menu's Save As command.

When you choose the Save As command, Excel displays the dialog box shown in Figure 1.6. To specify the drive for storing your worksheet file, move the selection cursor to the Drives box, activate the drop down list, and select the correct drive. Use the Directories list box to choose the directory or subdirectory where you want to store your worksheet.

FIGURE 1.6:

The File Save As dialog box

Name your worksheet file by moving the selection cursor to the File Name text box and typing the name. Let's use BUDGET as the name for your sample worksheet. We'll be using this worksheet in the next lesson. Don't enter a file extension. Excel automatically adds an .XLS extension to all your worksheet files.

When your File Save As dialog box is complete, select the OK command button to save the BUDGET.XLS worksheet. Once you've saved and named a worksheet file, you can use the Save command on the File menu or the Save File tool on the tool bar for subsequent saves.

The Options command button on the File Save As dialog box opens the door to some useful features such as automatic file backup, passwords, and read-only files. See your Excel documentation for more information.

EXITING THE PROGRAM

Once you've saved your work you can exit Excel by choosing the Exit command from the File menu. Windows closes the Excel application window and redisplays the Excel 4 program group window.

To exit Windows, choose Exit from the program group File menu.

LOOKING AHEAD

Lesson 1 helped you get off to a fast start by showing you how to create and save your first Excel worksheet. For further information on these subjects and some of Excel's advanced features, see the following topics in the Reference section of this book.

Analysis Tools for Special Uses

Arranging Window Size and Position

Cell Protection

Help for Lotus 1-2-3 Users

Help for Microsoft Multiplan Users

Learning Microsoft Excel

Optimization Modeling

Pasting Functions in Formulas

Protecting Documents

Saving Files in a Workbook

Series Values

Table Command Scenarios

Target Value Modeling

Viewing Document Window Formats

What-If Modeling

Excel also provides some powerful tools for editing and enhancing your worksheets. Lesson 2 is designed to help you quickly build a solid framework of editing skills.

TWO

Building a Framework of Editing Skills

INTRODUCING

Retrieving saved worksheets

Undoing your mistakes

Working with and editing ranges

Inserting and deleting cells, rows, and columns

Using the Find and Replace commands

Spell-checking your worksheet

Excel has many helpful commands such as Clear, Copy, Paste, Cut, Fill, Insert, Delete, Find, Replace, Undo, and Spelling that make editing your worksheets easier and more efficient. Let's retrieve your BUDGET.XLS worksheet and explore some basic editing techniques.

RETRIEVING YOUR WORKSHEET

To retrieve the BUDGET.XLS worksheet you created and saved in Lesson 1, start Excel and select the Open command from the File menu or the Open File tool from the tool bar. Excel displays the File Open dialog box shown in Figure 2.1.

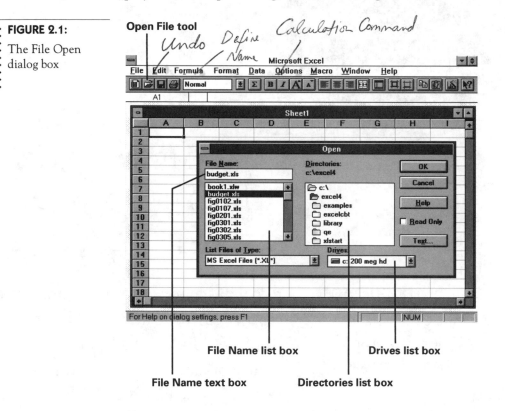

FIGURE 2.1:

The File Open dialog box

File Name list box

Drives list box

File Name text box

Directories list box

Specify the disk you saved your worksheet on by activating the Drives drop down list box and selecting the correct drive. Use the Directories list box to select the directory in which your file is stored.

To identify the BUDGET.XLS worksheet file, enter the file name in the File Name text box, or select the file from the File Name list box. Select the OK command button to retrieve your worksheet.

UNDERSTANDING WORKSHEET RECALCULATION

As you edit your worksheet, Excel automatically updates the formulas and recalculates the result. The mouse pointer changes to an hourglass symbol when recalculation takes place. If you resume work, Excel suspends recalculation until you're finished. The word "Calculate" is displayed on the status bar when your worksheet needs to be recalculated.

You can force recalculation by pressing F9 or selecting the Calculate Now command button on the Calculation dialog box. To display the Calculation dialog box, choose the Calculation command from the Options menu.

UNDOING MISTAKES

If you make a mistake entering data or editing your worksheet, you can use the Edit menu's Undo command to reverse the effects of your last action. You can even undo an undo operation.

Experiment with the Undo command as you practice the various editing commands in this lesson. Remember, Undo can only undo your last action.

WARNING

Undo cannot undo everything. It won't undo the File Delete, Data Delete, and Data Extract commands.

WORKING WITH RANGES

Ranges are rectangular portions of your worksheet. The smallest possible range is a single cell and the largest is your entire worksheet. You can define a range of any size to make editing faster and more efficient.

Select a single-cell range with the cell selector. Multiple-cell ranges can be selected by placing the mouse pointer on one of the range's corners, holding down the left mouse button, and dragging the pointer to the opposite corner. Using the navigation keys, move the cell selector to the top left corner of the range, hold down the Shift key, and move the selector to the bottom right corner.

To make working with ranges easier, Excel lets you assign names to ranges and identify them by name instead of by range address. To name a range, first select it, and then select the Formula menu's Define Name command to display the dialog box shown in Figure 2.2.

Enter your range name in the Name text box and press Enter. Your name should begin with a letter and not use any spaces. Named ranges are listed in the Names in Sheet box and the cell address of the selected named range is displayed in the Refers To box.

ERASING RANGES

You can erase single-cell and multiple-cell ranges quickly and easily. Let's erase range A6:C6 in your worksheet by selecting it with the navigation keys or the mouse, and then pressing the Del key or choosing the Clear command from the Edit menu.

Pressing the right mouse button displays a Shortcuts menu of frequently used commands such as Clear, Copy, Paste, Cut, Insert, and Delete. As you practice the editing tasks in this lesson, use the Shortcuts menu to build your level of speed and efficiency.

Excel displays the Clear dialog box shown in Figure 2.3. Four erasure options are listed with Formulas as the default option.

:
: **FIGURE 2.3:**
:
: Range A6:C6
: selected and the
: Clear dialog box
:

The Formats option button erases just the range formatting, the Formulas option erases all the cell data, and Notes erases notes created with the Formula Note command. The All option button erases everything.

Leaving the default setting for Formulas activated, select OK to complete the erasure. Figure 2.4 shows your sample worksheet with range A6:C6 cleared.

FIGURE 2.4:

The worksheet with range A6:C6 cleared

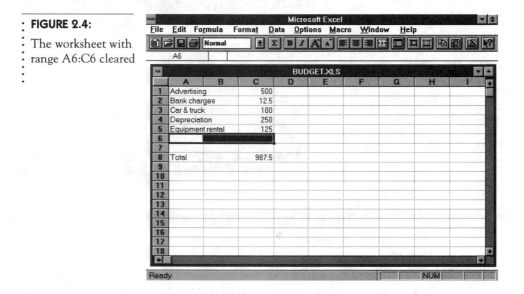

COPYING, CUTTING, AND PASTING

You can copy or cut the contents of cells and ranges, and paste them in other locations. Let's copy the range C1:C5 and paste it in both columns D and E.

To begin, select the range C1:C5, and then choose the Copy command from the Edit menu. You can also press the right mouse button and select Copy from the Shortcuts menu. Excel displays a flashing marquee around the range selected for copying.

Next, select the entire destination range, D1:E5, or just the first row of the range, D1:E1. Choose the Paste command from the Edit menu or Shortcuts menu, and Excel pastes the contents and format of the copied cells in the selected location.

Figure 2.5 shows how your worksheet should look after completing the copy and paste operation. When you select a destination range that is larger by a number of exact sizes than the copied multiple-cell range, the paste operation will automatically duplicate the original range the number of times it takes to fill the destination range.

Fill

: **FIGURE 2.5:**
: The worksheet with
: two copies of C1:C5
: pasted in D1:E5

Microsoft Excel
File Edit Formula Format Data Options Macro Window Help

D1 | 500

BUDGET.XLS

	A	B	C	D	E	F	G	H	I
1	Advertising		500	500	500				
2	Bank charges		12.5	12.5	12.5				
3	Car & truck		100	100	100				
4	Depreciation		250	250	250				
5	Equipment rental		125	125	125				
6									
7									
8	Total		987.5						
9									
10									
11									
12									
13									
14									
15									
16									
17									
18									

Select destination and press ENTER or choose Paste | NUM

When you repeat the process just outlined, choosing the Cut command instead of the Copy command, the selected range is removed or "cut" from its original location before you paste it in a new location.

If you paste a copy of a single-cell range into a multiple-cell range, the contents of the single cell are duplicated in each cell in the destination range. You only need select the top left corner of the destination range when you're pasting a copy of a multiple-cell range into another multiple-cell range of the same size.

When you copy a formula, Excel adjusts the relative cell references used in that formula. The formula =C1+C2+C3+C4+C5 in your sample worksheet adds the first set of budget numbers. If you copy this formula from cell C8 to cell D8, Excel automatically adjusts the cell references to =D1+D2+D3+D4+D5. Cell references are also adjusted when you copy a formula to a different row. To prevent Excel from automatically adjusting the relative references of copied formulas, you can make them absolute. Simply place a dollar sign ($) in front of the parts of your formula you wish to retain as absolute. For more information on relative and absolute references, consult your Excel documentation.

FILLING RANGES

The Edit menu's Fill commands let you copy a label, value or formula either vertically or horizontally into adjacent cells. To copy across a row or down a column, select the cell you want to copy as well as the cells you want to fill, and then choose the Fill Down or Fill Right command from the Edit menu. If you press the Shift key and then access the Edit menu, Excel displays the Fill Left and Fill Up commands.

TIP

A selected cell or range displays a "handle" at its lower-right corner. You can enlarge or contract the selected area by placing your mouse pointer on the handle, holding down the left mouse button, and dragging the corner in the desired direction. If you take the time to experiment with these commands and use your sample worksheet, be sure to retain a version of BUDGET.XLS that resembles Figure 2.5. We'll be using this worksheet in subsequent exercises.

WORKING WITH CELLS, ROWS, AND COLUMNS

Excel lets you insert and delete cells, rows, and columns on your worksheet with speed and efficiency. You can easily delete what you no longer need, or insert new items between existing entries when you need to expand your worksheet.

THE INSERT COMMAND

To insert a row, click on any cell in the row below where you want a row inserted. To insert a column, click on any cell in the column to the right of where you want a column inserted.

To insert a cell in a column, select the cell above where the new cell should go. To insert a cell in a row, select the cell to the left of where you want the cell inserted.

When you choose the Insert command, Excel displays the Insert dialog box shown in Figure 2.6.

Mark the Entire Row or Entire Column option buttons to insert these items, or the Shift Cells Right or Shift Cells Down buttons to insert cells. When you've marked the appropriate option button, select OK.

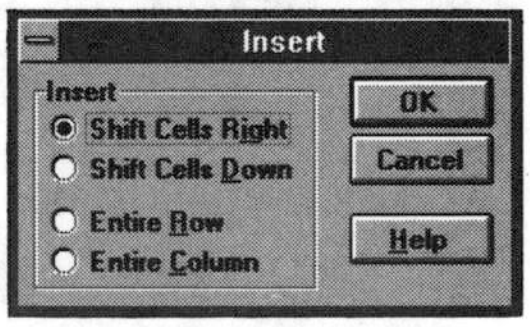

FIGURE 2.6:

The Insert dialog box

Insert
Insert
● Shift Cells Right
○ Shift Cells Down
○ Entire Row
○ Entire Column
OK
Cancel
Help

THE DELETE COMMAND

To delete a cell, row, or column, click on the specific cell, or any cell in the row or column you wish to delete, and choose the Delete command from the Edit menu or the Shortcuts menu. Excel displays the dialog box shown in Figure 2.7.

To complete the operation, mark the appropriate options in the dialog box and select OK.

A faster way to insert or delete one or more complete rows or columns is to select and highlight the rows or columns by clicking on their numbers or letters in the worksheet borders, and then choosing the command. Remember that Excel inserts rows above the first selected row, and columns to the left of the first selected column. Cells are inserted to the left of selected cells in a row and above selected cells in a column.

FIGURE 2.7:

The Delete
dialog box

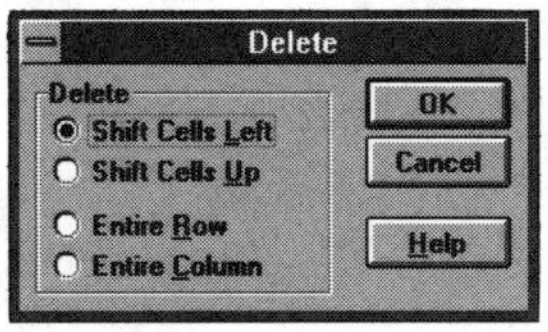

USING FIND AND REPLACE

Excel provides two commands that search your worksheet for specific entries. The Find command simply locates what you're looking for. The Replace command not only finds it, but gives you the option of replacing it with a new label, value, or formula.

THE FIND COMMAND

To search your worksheet and locate specific entries, choose the Find command on the Formula menu. Excel displays the dialog box shown in Figure 2.8.

FIGURE 2.8:

The Find dialog box

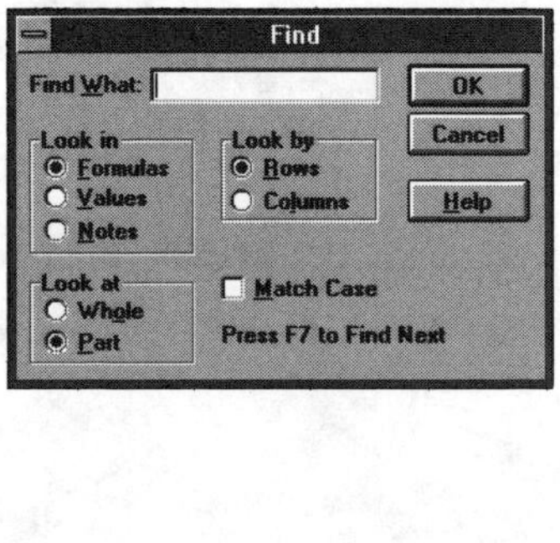

Enter the label, value, or formula you want to search for in the Find What text box, mark the appropriate option buttons and check box to specify the parameters of your search, and then select OK to begin.

If Excel finds an entry that matches your search parameters, it moves the cell selector to that cell. To resume searching, press F7.

THE REPLACE COMMAND

When you choose the Replace command, Excel displays the dialog box shown in Figure 2.9.

Enter the item you want to find, and also the label, value, or formula you want to replace it with. Mark option buttons and check box as appropriate.

Use the Replace All button to tell Excel to automatically find and replace all the items you've designated. The Find Next and Replace buttons allow you to replace found entries on an individual basis. The Close button stops the operation.

You can streamline your find and replace efforts with large or complex worksheets by first selecting the specific range you want to search. If you don't select a range before you begin, Excel searches your entire worksheet.

FIGURE 2.9:

The Replace
dialog box

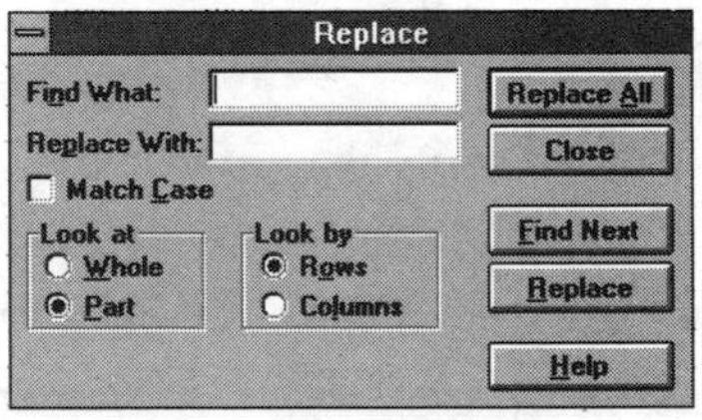

CHECKING YOUR SPELLING

Excel lets you check the spelling of a selected word, a selected range, or all the words on your worksheet. Choose the Spelling command from the Options menu to start the Spelling function and display the Spelling dialog box shown in Figure 2.10.

When you first use the Spelling command, Excel asks your permission to create a dictionary file named CUSTOM.DIC. This file is used to store your personal preferences.

: **FIGURE 2.10:**
: The Spelling
: dialog box

Excel finds and displays words that are not in its dictionary. If the spelling is correct, select the Ignore or Ignore All button. If you select the Suggest button, Excel creates a list of suggestions.

Checking the Always Suggest box tells Excel to make suggestions automatically. Excel also ignores words in all uppercase if you check that box.

To correct a word, type the correct spelling in the Change To text box or select one of Excel's suggestions, and then select the Change or Change All buttons. To add words to your personal dictionary (CUSTOM.DIC) or another dictionary listed in the Add Words To box, select the Add button.

To stop the spell-checking process, select the Cancel button. When the checking operation is allowed to run, the Cancel button changes to the Close button. Select the Close button when you're finished checking your spelling.

LOOKING AHEAD

Lesson 2 has provided you with a quick overview of Excel's basic editing features. For further information on these subjects and some of Excel's advanced features, see the following topics in the Reference section of this book.

Calculating Worksheets

Clearing Unwanted Data

Consolidating Data

Naming Ranges

Outlining Worksheet Data

Pasting Link Formulas

Pasting Special Clipboard Data

Repeating the Last Command

Replacing Cell Data

Selecting Special Cell Characteristics

Series Values

Lesson 3 shows you how to enhance your worksheets with a formidable array of formatting tools. If you plan to take a break at this point, be sure to save your worksheet before you exit the program.

ENHANCING YOUR WORK WITH FORMATTING

INTRODUCING

*Excel's AutoFormat
Command*

Aligning labels and values

*Assigning formats
to numbers*

*Changing font styles
and sizes*

*Creating borders and
shaded cells*

*Modifying column and
row size*

With proper formatting, your worksheets are easier to read and more visually attractive. This lesson puts you on the fast track to enhancing your work with Excel's formatting features. If you haven't already done so, start Excel and retrieve your BUDGET.XLS worksheet

USING THE AUTOFORMAT COMMAND

Excel's AutoFormat feature performs many standard formatting tasks in a single operation. Like most of Excel's basic features, Autoformat can be accessed with a menu command or by selecting it from the tool bar.

To use the AutoFormat command, first select the worksheet range you want to format. Choose AutoFormat from the Format menu, and Excel displays the dialog box shown in Figure 3.1.

FIGURE 3.1:

The AutoFormat dialog box.

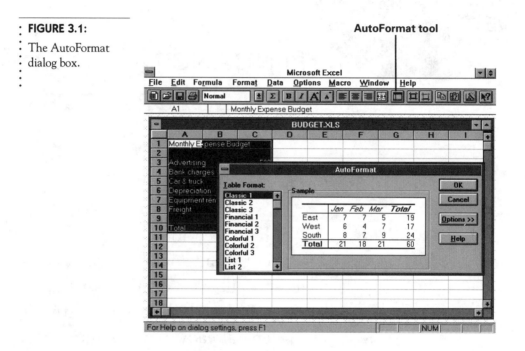

You can choose each of Excel's AutoFormats from the Table Format list and observe its effect in the Sample box. To apply an AutoFormat to your worksheet, select the OK button. To apply your selected AutoFormat style to another range on your worksheet, use the AutoFormat tool on the tool bar.

For more information on the many AutoFormat options you can access with the Options button on the dialog box, consult your Excel documentation.

WORKING WITH MANUAL FORMATTING

As you learn to create more complex and specialized worksheets, your formatting efforts require similar treatment. The following sections detail each of Excel's specific formatting features. Like the AutoFormat Command, each feature can usually be accessed from a menu as well as the toolbar.

ALIGNING LABELS AND VALUES

Excel normally aligns values against the right edge of a cell and labels against the left edge. You can override these default alignments by using the Left Align, Center, Right Align, and Center Across tools on the tool bar.

Let's enter a label in cell A1 and then center it across the range A1:C1 on your Budget.XLS worksheet. First select the range A1:C1, and then select the Center Across tool. Figure 3.2 shows your worksheet after this alignment. The Center tool only centers a label or value in a single cell.

FIGURE 3.2:

The label centered across range A1:C1

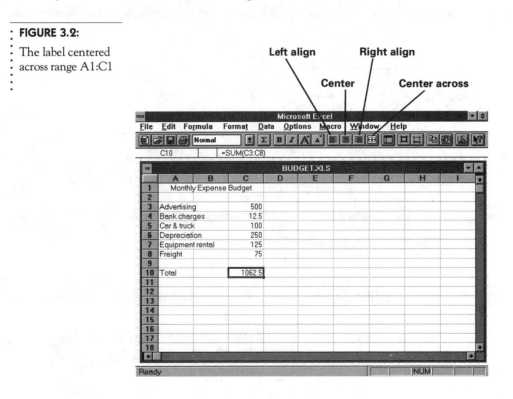

You can access a more sophisticated array of alignment features by choosing the Alignment command from the Format or Shortcuts menu. Excel displays the Alignment dialog box shown in Figure 3.3.

The General setting is the default for horizontal alignment. Fill repeats a label or value as many times as it will fit in a cell. If there are empty cells to the right of a cell and you've assigned them the Fill alignment, they're also filled. Justify aligns your text both left and right when the Wrap Text box is checked.

FIGURE 3.3:

The Alignment dialog box

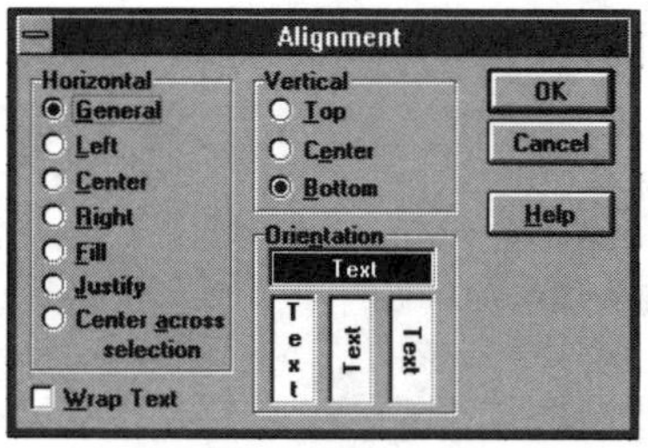

The Vertical option buttons affect label and value alignment as described. The vertical alignment default setting is Bottom.

The Orientation buttons rotate selected labels and values as shown.

WARNING

You may need to adjust row height in your selected range to accommodate rotated text. This topic is covered later in this lesson.

ASSIGNING FORMATS TO NUMBERS

You can assign numeric formats such as dollar signs, percentage symbols, and commas by using the Number command or the tool bar's Style box. Choose the Number command from the Format or Shortcuts menu to display the Number Format dialog box shown in Figure 3.4.

The Category box shows the seven available formats, with All as the default setting. The Format Codes demonstrate the appearance of options. General is the

FIGURE 3.4:

The Number Format dialog box

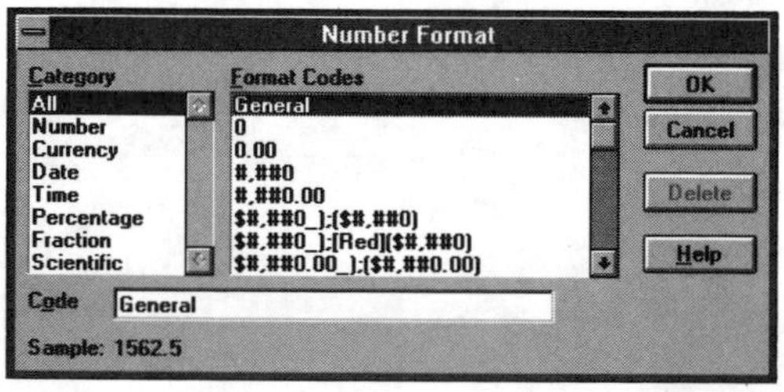

default setting, and the Sample text box shows how the value in the active cell appears when formatted with this code.

You can also use the Code text box to create custom formatting codes. Refer to your Excel documentation for information on this subject.

Choose the $#,##0_);($#,###0) code and apply it to your worksheet by selecting the OK button. Figure 3.5 shows the result. Note the location of the tool bar Style box.

FIGURE 3.5:

Your worksheet with
formatted numbers

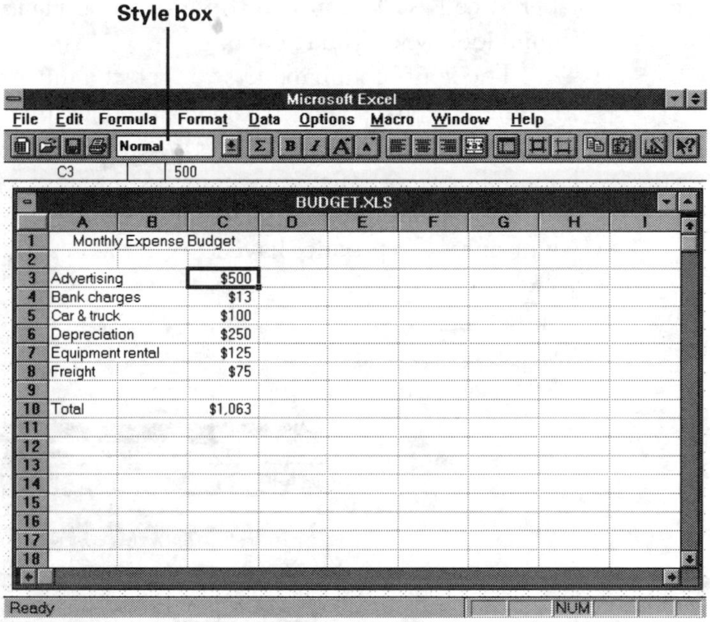

Style box

	A	B	C	D	E	F	G	H	I
1	Monthly Expense Budget								
2									
3	Advertising		$500						
4	Bank charges		$13						
5	Car & truck		$100						
6	Depreciation		$250						
7	Equipment rental		$125						
8	Freight		$75						
9									
10	Total		$1,063						

The fastest way to format numbers is with the Style box on the tool bar. The default setting is Normal, but when you activate the drop down list box, six additional formats are displayed.

If you have the time, feel free to experiment with the various formatting options we've covered so far. Remember, you can use the Undo command to undo your last action. Be sure to retain a version of your worksheet similar to the one shown in Figure 3.5. We'll be using this worksheet for later exercises.

CHANGING FONT STYLES AND SIZES

Excel offers you a wide variety of choices for selecting the best font styles and sizes for your worksheet. There are four font tools on Excel's tool bar for making quick changes to bold or italic text, larger or smaller point sizes.

Points are used to measure font sizes. A point is one-seventy-second of an inch. Common point sizes include 8, 10, 12, 14, 18, 24. Excel's default setting is 10 point Helvetica.

Select the label in range A1:C1, and then the Bold and Italic tools. Next select the label in cell A10, and then the Italic tool. Figure 3.6 shows how your worksheet should look when you're done.

The Fonts command lets you select a full array of font characteristics including different type styles, strikeouts and underlines, and a variety of colors. Choose the Font command from the Format menu or the Shortcuts menu to display the Font dialog box shown in Figure 3.7.

Type styles other than Helvetica can be selected from the Font list box. Fonts your printer can produce have a printer icon next to them. The Font Style box lets

---

FIGURE 3.6:

Your worksheet with bold and italic labels

Italic Bold Next size larger Next size smaller

	A	B	C	D	E	F	G	H	I
1	*Monthly Expense Budget*								
2									
3	Advertising		$500						
4	Bank charges		$13						
5	Car & truck		$100						
6	Depreciation		$250						
7	Equipment rental		$125						
8	Freight		$75						
9									
10	*Total*		$1,063						

C10 =SUM(C3:C8)

BUDGET.XLS

Microsoft Excel

File Edit Formula Format Data Options Macro Window Help

Ready NUM

FIGURE 3.7:

The Font dialog box

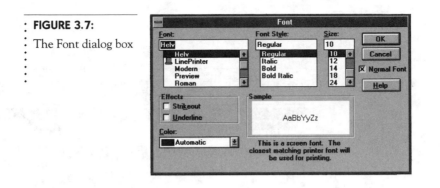

you choose Regular, Italic, Bold, or Bold Italic. To change point sizes, use the Size list box.

Special effects, such as Strikeout and Underline, are activated by their check boxes. Colors other than Automatic, which is black, can be selected from the Color drop down list box. The Sample text box shows an example of the current font selection, and the Normal Font check box resets the default to 10 point Helvetica regular.

As noted on the Font dialog box, Excel prints your worksheet with the closest matching printer font if your printer won't support your font selection. What you see on your screen may not be what you get on your printed documents. See your Excel documentation for more information on installing and using fonts.

CREATING BORDERS AND SHADED CELLS

One of Excel's niftier features allows you to create lines and shading that help organize, clarify, and emphasize the information on your worksheet. Choose the Border command from the Format or Shortcuts menu to display the dialog box shown in Figure 3.8. Notice the Draw Box and Draw Line tools on the tool bar.

Select one of the Border option buttons to designate the line location on your selected worksheet range, and one of the Style buttons to select a variety of thicknesses, dashed, or double line styles. To select a color other than black, activate the color list box.

To shade the cells in your selected range, mark the Shade check box.

To change Excel's default shading style and color, choose the Patterns command from the Format or Shortcuts menu to display the Patterns dialog box.

FIGURE 3.8:

The Border dialog box

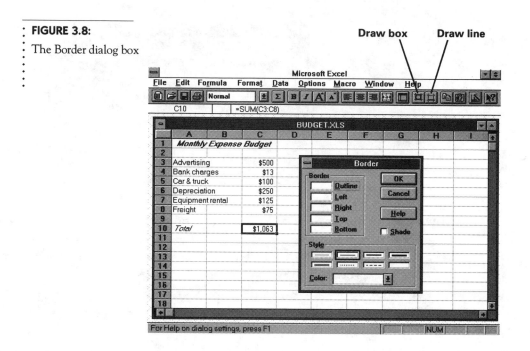

Draw box   Draw line

For quicker formatting, Excel provides two line drawing tools on the tool bar. The Draw Box tool creates an outside border around a selected worksheet range, and the Draw Line tool draws a line along the bottom edge of a selected range.

MODIFYING COLUMN AND ROW SIZE

As you reformat the labels and values in your worksheet, you may need to modify the standard column and row sizes to accommodate your formatting changes. The Row Height and Column Width commands allow you to make precise adjustments to these dimensions, and also hide and unhide selected columns or rows.

The easiest way to modify a column or row dimension is to point your mouse to the right edge of the letter border for the column you want to change, or to the bottom edge of the number border for the row you want to change. When the mouse pointer changes to a two-sided arrow, hold down the left mouse button and drag the edge of the column or row to create the desired dimension.

Choose the Row Height command from the Format menu to display the dialog box shown in Figure 3.9.

To change the height of a selected row, enter the desired height in points. Mark the Standard Height check box to reset the 12.75 point default. To unhide a row you selected to hide, select a range that includes the rows above and below the hidden row, and then select the Unhide button.

The Column Width command on the Format menu displays the dialog box in Figure 3.10.

FIGURE 3.9:

The Row Height
dialog box

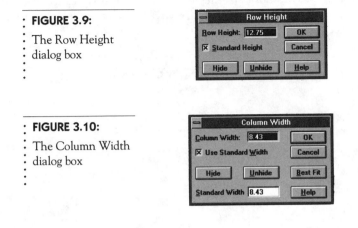

FIGURE 3.10:

The Column Width
dialog box

Enter the desired column width in characters, or select the Best Fit button for automatic adjustment to the widest label or value. Mark the Use Standard Width box to reset the default to 8.43 characters. To unhide a column, select the range of columns including those to the left and right of the hidden column, and then select the Unhide button.

You can also sort the cells in selected columns or rows of your worksheet and arrange the values they contain in ascending or descending order. The Sort command on the Data menu displays a dialog box that lets you define the parameters of sorting operations. For more information on sorting, see Lesson 7.

LOOKING AHEAD

Lesson 3 has demonstrated some basic tools for making your worksheets easier to read and more visually attractive. For more information on the subjects introduced in this lesson, consult the following topics in the Reference section of this book.

Bordering and Shading Cells and Ranges

Color Palette for Document Windows

Drawing Features

Justifying Text

Patterns and Cell Shading

Sorting Worksheet Data

Styles for Worksheet Formatting

Lesson 4 provides some valuable insights and practical information on printing and managing your files. If you plan to take a break at this point, be sure to save your worksheet before you exit the program.

Printing and Managing Your Files

INTRODUCING

Printing with Excel

The Page Setup and Print Preview commands

The Options menu printing commands

Managing multiple files in memory

Deleting files

Exporting and importing files

Printing with Excel is faster and easier than with most other popular spreadsheet programs. Excel also has several unique and convenient file management features that allow you to work with more than one file at a time, and import or export a variety of other types of document files. Let's take a quick look at these functions. If you haven't already done so, start Excel and retrieve your BUDGET.XLS worksheet

PRINTING WITH EXCEL

To print your BUDGET.XLS worksheet, choose the Print command from the File menu or select the Print tool from the tool bar. Excel displays the dialog box shown in Figure 4.1.

The Print dialog box lets you print a specific range of pages, select an appropriate print quality, and enter the number of copies you want. You can also mark various boxes or buttons to print just your worksheet, cell notes only, or both.

FIGURE 4.1:

The Print dialog box

Print tool

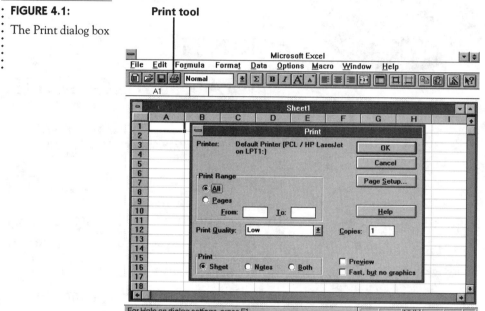

THE PAGE SETUP COMMAND

When you select the Setup button on the Print dialog box or choose the Page Setup command from the File menu, Excel displays the dialog box shown in Figure 4.2.

The Orientation option buttons allow you to select a standard portrait or a horizontal landscape orientation for your printed worksheet pages. You can choose a paper size appropriate for your printer by activating the Paper Size list box. The Margins text boxes let you enter your preferences in inches, and the Center check boxes center your printed worksheet horizontally or vertically between your chosen margins.

FIGURE 4.2:

The Page Setup
dialog box

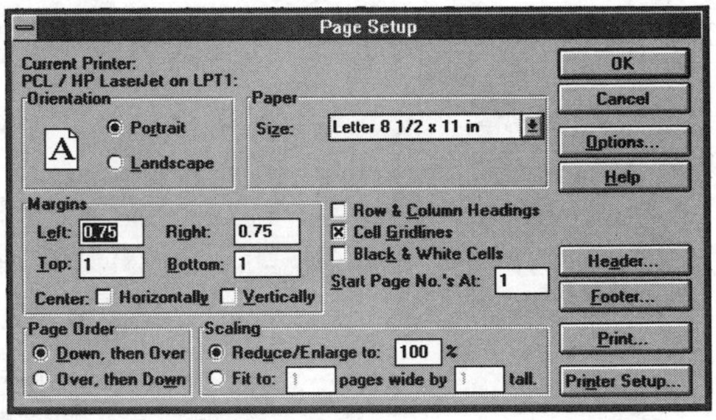

The Row & Column Headings check box prints the column letter and row number borders. Marking the Cell Gridlines check box prints the gridlines between worksheet cells. The Black & White Cells check box prints colored cells in black and white, and the Start Page No.'s At text box lets you choose and enter a number for the first page of your printed worksheet.

To print and break your worksheet pages by columns, mark the Down, then Over option button. To print and break your worksheet pages by rows, mark the Over, then Down button. The Scaling option buttons and text boxes let you size your worksheet by a specified percentage or to fit a specific number of pages.

The Chart Size option buttons on the Page Setup dialog box control chart printing. Refer to Lesson 5 for more information on Excel's charting features.

The Page Setup dialog box also has several command buttons. The Options button displays a dialog box for choosing the options supported by your active printer. The Header and Footer buttons display dialog boxes for adding or changing these items at the top and bottom margins on each of your printed pages. The Print button prints your worksheet, and the Printer Setup button displays a dialog box for changing the active printer.

As you learn about Excel's wide variety of printing and page setup options, use your BUDGET.XLS worksheet to experiment with them and view the printed results. We'll be creating other sample worksheets in subsequent lessons so you needn't retain a saved version of BUDGET.XLS.

THE PRINT PREVIEW COMMAND

Choose the Print Preview command from the File menu or select Preview from the Print dialog box. Excel displays a print preview of your BUDGET.XLS worksheet as shown in Figure 4.3. To make it easier to view the content of our sample worksheet, the Cell Gridlines check box on the Page Setup dialog box has been left unmarked.

· **FIGURE 4.3:**
· The Print Preview
· window

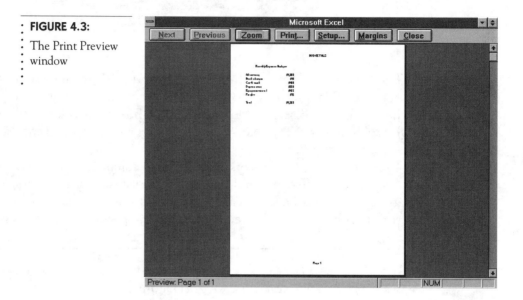

The Print Preview Window has seven command buttons. Next and Previous allow you to page back and forth through multipage worksheet files. The Zoom button enlarges the previewed page to fill the window as in Figure 4.4.

If you're using a mouse, the mouse pointer becomes a magnifying glass symbol. You can zoom in on specific portions of your worksheet by pointing the magnifying glass symbol and clicking the left mouse button.

The Print button prints your worksheet, Setup displays the Page Setup dialog box, and the Margins button displays the dashed margin lines shown in Figure 4.5. You can change your page margins by moving these lines with your mouse.

To remove the Print Preview Window, select the Close button.

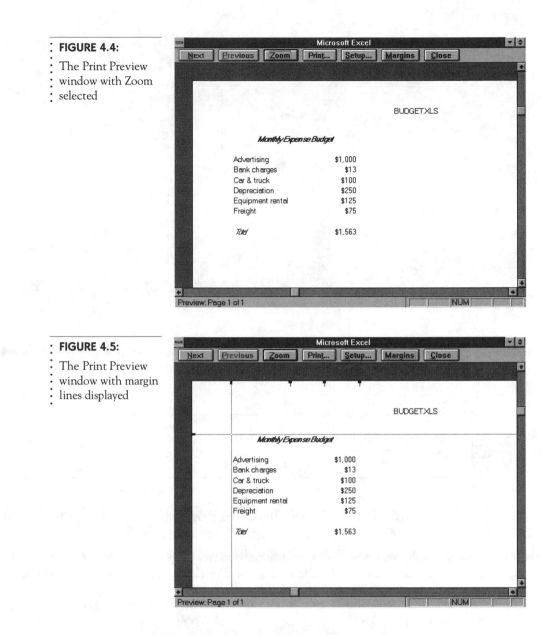

FIGURE 4.4:

The Print Preview window with Zoom selected

FIGURE 4.5:

The Print Preview window with margin lines displayed

OPTIONS MENU PRINT COMMANDS

When you activate Excel's Options menu, as shown in Figure 4.6, three additional printing options are made available.

Set Print Area To set a specific area of your worksheet for printing, first select the range you want printed, and then choose Set Print Area from the Options menu. Excel draws dashed lines along the print area's borders, and when you use

FIGURE 4.6:

The Options menu print commands

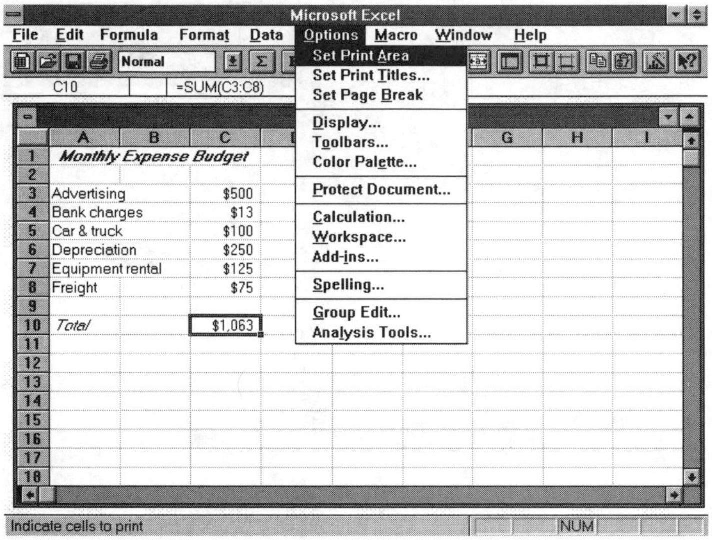

![Microsoft Excel screenshot showing the Options menu open with commands including Set Print Area, Set Print Titles, Set Page Break, Display, Toolbars, Color Palette, Protect Document, Calculation, Workspace, Add-ins, Spelling, Group Edit, and Analysis Tools. The worksheet shows a Monthly Expense Budget with Advertising $500, Bank charges $13, Car & truck $100, Depreciation $250, Equipment rental $125, Freight $75, and Total $1,063.]

the File menu's Print command, Excel prints only the range you set as the print area. To change the print area, select a new worksheet range, and then reactivate the Set Print Area command.

To remove the set print area and make your entire worksheet available for printing, you can use the Define Name command on the Formula menu.

Set Print Titles

When working with large worksheets that need more than one page for printing, you may want to designate a particular row or column to appear as a title on each printed page of your worksheet. Choose the Set Print Titles command from the Options menu to display the dialog box shown in Figure 4.7.

Enter the row or column range address you want to use in the appropriate text box. You don't need to enter all the letters and numbers in the range definition, but you should make your definition absolute. To set row 1 as a horizontal print title, enter the definition **$1:$1**. To set column A as a vertical print title, enter the definition **$A:$A**.

FIGURE 4.7:

The Set Print Titles dialog box

[Set Print Titles dialog box with Print Titles section containing Titles for Columns: and Titles for Rows: text boxes, and OK, Cancel, Help buttons.]

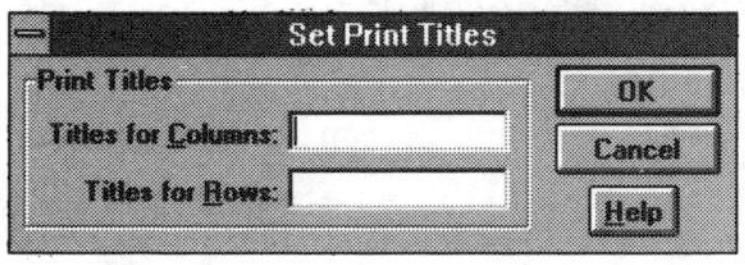

The fastest way to set print titles is to first select a row or column by clicking on its number or letter in the row or column border, and then choose the Set Print Titles command. To select a row and column for both horizontal and vertical print titles, first select the row, and then select the column while holding down the Ctrl key.

Set Page Break Excel automatically breaks pages as they are normally filled in printing. To force Excel to set a page break at a specific location on your worksheet, first select the column or row that follows the place you want the break, and then choose the Set Page Break command from the Options menu. To remove a set page break, select the column or row that follows the break, and then choose the Remove Page Break command on the Options menu.

MANAGING YOUR FILES WITH EXCEL

Excel lets you work with more than one worksheet file at a time, and export and import files to and from other applications. All of these capabilities can be accessed through the File menu. Let's briefly discuss each of them.

HANDLING MULTIPLE FILES

When you start Excel, an empty worksheet file named SHEET1.XLS is automatically opened. To open an existing worksheet file, use the Open command on the File menu. To open additional blank worksheets, use the File menu's New command.

When you choose the New command, Excel displays the dialog box shown in Figure 4.8. Select the file type from the list box and then OK. When you use the New worksheet tool on the tool bar, Excel displays a new worksheet file.

Each of your open files is displayed in a separate document window, and each window is listed as an option on Excel's Window menu. To activate a window, select it from the Window menu. To remove an active window, choose the File menu's Close command. If your worksheet has been changed and isn't flagged as read only, Excel asks if you want to save your changes before closing.

To close all your open worksheet files, press and hold the Shift key while activating the File menu. Excel replaces the File menu's Close command with the Close All command.

FIGURE 4.8:

The New dialog box

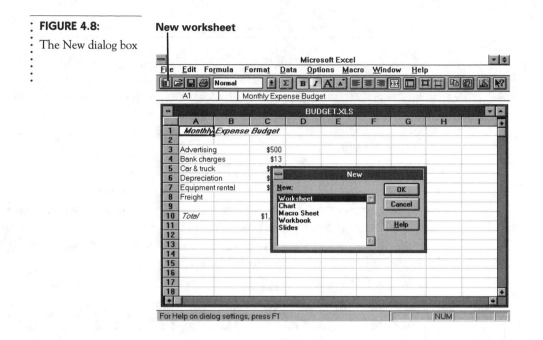

DELETING FILES

To erase Excel files you no longer need, choose the Delete command from the File menu to display the dialog box shown in Figure 4.9.

Use the Drives and Directory list boxes, and the File Name text box or File Name list to locate and identify the specific file you want to delete. When the dialog box is complete, select OK.

Refer to Lessons 1 and 2 for detailed discussions on how to use the various Drives, Directory, and File Name boxes on the File Save As and File Open dialog boxes. These features operate in a similar way on the Delete Document dialog box.

FIGURE 4.9:

The Delete Document dialog box

EXPORTING AND IMPORTING

To create a worksheet file you can export to another application, choose the File menu's Save As command to display the File Save As dialog box. Activate the Save File as Type list, shown in Figure 4.10, and select the type of file you want to create.

There are almost two dozen export file formats available for different kinds of Excel files. SYLK files are standard ASCII formatted database files that let you easily exchange spreadsheets between different operating systems, such as DOS to Macintosh, with formats and formulas intact. For more information on choosing the correct export file types, refer to your Excel documentation.

To retrieve a worksheet file originally created by another application, choose the Open command from the File menu to display the File Open dialog box. Activate the List Files of Type list, shown in Figure 4.11, and select the type of file you want to retrieve or import.

FIGURE 4.10:

The Save File as Type list

FIGURE 4.11:

The List Files of Type list

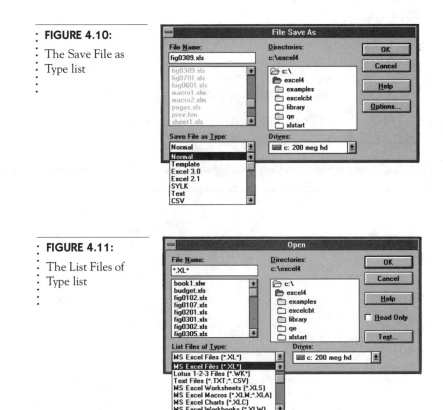

If you're attempting to import a text file, you can let Excel apply a default set of assumptions to the file or you can select the Text command button on the File Open dialog box. Excel displays a Text File Options dialog box that lets you describe the text file's column delimiters and the system that created the file.

LOOKING AHEAD

This lesson has taught you the basic printing and file management skills you need to get the most from Excel in the shortest period of time. For more information on the subjects introduced in this lesson, the following topics are covered in the Reference section of this book.

Freezing Panes on Split Document Windows

Hiding Document Windows

Linking Files

New Windows

Notes on Cells

Parsing Imported Text

Print Report

Splitting Windows into Panes

Unhiding Document Windows

The next lesson advances your level of skill even further, with a quick introduction to Excel's powerful charting features.

LESSON
FIVE

PRESENTING YOUR DATA WITH CHARTS

INTRODUCING

*Creating charts with the
ChartWizard*

*Formatting with the
Chart tool bar*

*Saving charts as
independent files*

*Printing charts as
separate items*

Excel doesn't limit your ability to present information to the rows and columns of a worksheet. You can use the program's charting features to graphically represent your worksheet data in a variety of interesting ways.

CREATING AND WORKING WITH CHARTS

Excel lets you create a full range of charts, including line charts, area charts, bar and column charts, and pie charts. In this lesson you'll be creating a new worksheet to use as a sample document. If you have the BUDGET.XLS worksheet open on your screen, use the File menu's Close command to remove it, and then the New command or the tool bar's New File tool to open a blank worksheet. Otherwise, start Excel and a blank worksheet document is automatically displayed.

USING THE CHARTWIZARD

The easiest and most direct way to convert your worksheets to charts is with Excel's ChartWizard. Let's create a sample worksheet, and then explore Excel's quickest and most convenient charting method step-by-step.

Take a few minutes to build the sample worksheet shown in Figure 5.1. It represents three years of revenue and expense data. When you've entered your data, use the File menu's Save As command to name your document SALES.XLS.

To chart worksheet data, you need to understand data series and data points. A data series is a set of one or more numeric values. In our sample SALES.XLS worksheet, the sales figures represent one data series and expenses are a second data series. The individual bits of data that make up a data series are called data points. If a data series consisted of three revenue figures for 1993, 1994, and 1995, the series would have three data points.

The ChartWizard converts your worksheets to charts in five simple steps. Dialog boxes appear at each step to guide you through the process. Note the location of the ChartWizard tool shown in Figure 5.1.

To begin, select the worksheet range you want to chart. Include any row or column headings in your selection. Select range A1:D3 on your sample worksheet.

Next, select the ChartWizard tool from the tool bar. Excel changes your mouse pointer to a cross hair. Point the cross hair to the upper left corner of where you want your chart placed, and then, holding down the left mouse button, drag the cross hair to where you want the lower right corner of your chart.

Excel draws a box to show the placement of your chart, and displays the first of five ChartWizard dialog boxes shown in Figure 5.2.

The ChartWizard lets you select a new range on your worksheet or enter a new range definition in the text box. To continue, select the Next button. Excel displays the second ChartWizard dialog box shown in Figure 5.3.

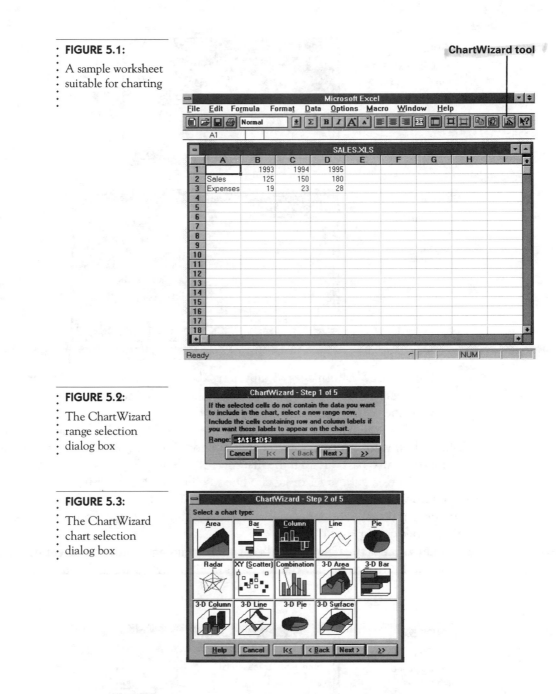

· FIGURE 5.1:
·
· A sample worksheet
· suitable for charting
·
·

ChartWizard tool

· FIGURE 5.2:
·
· The ChartWizard
· range selection
· dialog box
·

· FIGURE 5.3:
·
· The ChartWizard
· chart selection
· dialog box
·

You can select any chart type displayed on the dialog box. To continue with our example, select Line chart and then the Next button at the bottom of the dialog box. Excel displays the third ChartWizard dialog box shown in Figure 5.4.

Select the format you want for your Line chart by pointing to it, and then select the Next button. The fourth ChartWizard dialog box displays your sample Line chart as shown in Figure 5.5.

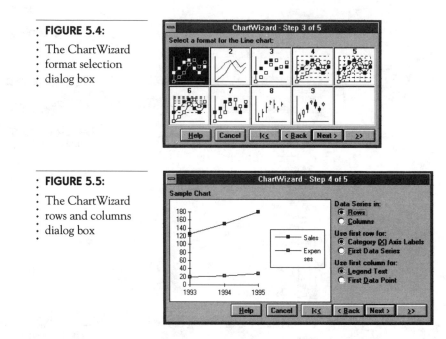

FIGURE 5.4:

The ChartWizard format selection dialog box

FIGURE 5.5:

The ChartWizard rows and columns dialog box

The ChartWizard makes assumptions about how you want your worksheet data displayed in a chart. If any of these assumptions are incorrect, you can change them with the option buttons on the dialog box.

The Data Series options let you tell the ChartWizard if your data series are displayed on your worksheet in rows or columns. The Use First Row (or Column) options tell the ChartWizard if the first row (or column) of your selected worksheet range contains a data series or labels. The Use First Column (or Row) options tell the ChartWizard if the first column (or row) of your selected worksheet range contains descriptions of the data series, referred to as legend text, or actually represents the first data point in the series.

Let's accept the ChartWizard's default settings and continue. Select the Next command button to display the fifth and final ChartWizard dialog box shown in Figure 5.6.

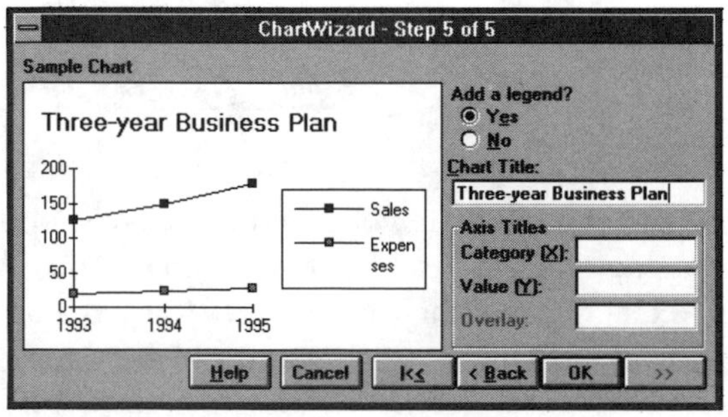

FIGURE 5.6:

The ChartWizard legends and titles dialog box

If you don't want the ChartWizard to include a legend on your chart, mark the No button.

If the first column or row of a data series includes descriptive text, such as the Sales and Expenses labels in our sample worksheet, the ChartWizard uses this text in the legend. Otherwise, the first data series is described as Series 1, the second as Series 2, and so on.

Let's add a title to your chart. Move the selection cursor to the Chart Title text box and enter the title shown in Figure 5.6. You can also add axis titles to your chart by entering the appropriate worksheet range for the horizontal, X-axis label in the Category text box, and the range for the vertical, Y-axis label in the Value text box. The Overlay text box is used when your chart has a second Y-axis.

To complete the process, select the OK command button at the bottom of the ChartWizard's fifth dialog box. Excel places the completed chart on your worksheet as shown in Figure 5.7.

You can easily move and resize a chart with your mouse. To move a chart, place the mouse pointer anywhere inside the chart and, holding down the left mouse button, drag it to the new location. To resize your chart, place the mouse pointer on one of the small square chart handles on the corners and along each side of the chart and, holding down the left mouse button, drag it until you've achieved the correct size and shape. This is a quick and effective way to adjust the chart size to accommodate the length of chart titles and labels.

FIGURE 5.7:
Your completed
Line chart

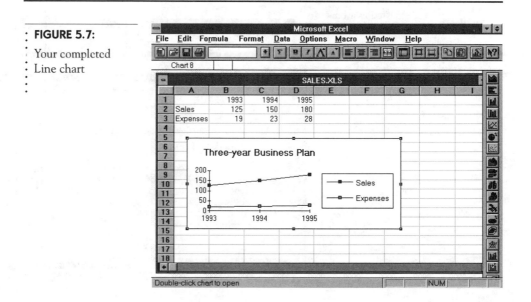

WORKING WITH THE CHART TOOL BAR

Once you've created a chart and placed it on your worksheet, Excel adds the Chart tool bar to your application window. You can use the various Chart tools to reformat and customize your chart.

If you don't want to use the Chart tool bar, place the mouse pointer on your worksheet and click the left mouse button. Excel removes the Chart tool bar, and any commands you choose now effect your worksheet, not your chart. To redisplay the Chart tool bar, simply click on your chart.

The majority of the buttons on the Chart tool bar change the format of your selected chart to the one illustrated on the button icon. Change the format of your Line chart by selecting the Bar chart tool. Your reformatted chart should look like Figure 5.8.

When you select the ChartWizard tool, the ChartWizard dialog boxes are displayed so you can modify your answers to the ChartWizard's questions. The Gridlines tool adds these features when the format of your chart accepts them. The Legend tool places a legend on your chart. To add arrows, which you can move around with your mouse, use the Arrow tool. Free Text lets you freely enter any new text into your chart.

FIGURE 5.8:
Your chart
reformatted as a Bar
chart

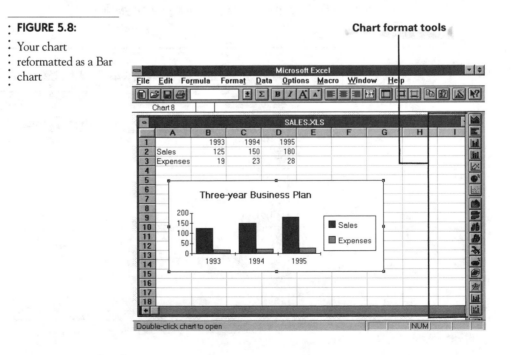

Take some time to experiment with each of the options offered by the ChartWizard's step-by-step dialog boxes. Sample the various formats and customizing tools on the Chart tool bar and view their effect on your sample SALES.XLS worksheet. Since we won't be using SALES.XLS in later lessons, you don't need to save a specific version of this worksheet.

Saving, Retrieving, and Printing Your Charts

The easiest way to save, retrieve, and print a chart is by letting it remain a part of your worksheet. You can also save, retrieve, and print your charts as independent files.

SAVING CHARTS AS INDEPENDENT FILES

To save your chart as an independent file, place your mouse pointer on it and double-click the left mouse button. Excel displays your chart in its own window as shown in Figure 5.9. Use the File menu's Save As command to name and save your chart.

To retrieve a chart saved as a separate file, simply use the Open command. Excel uses the file extension .XLC for charts.

FIGURE 5.9:
Your chart displayed in its own window

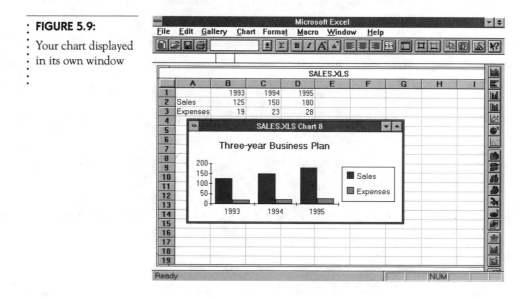

When you work with a chart in its own window, Excel displays a slightly different version of the menu bar including commands specifically related to charts. For more information on the special chart menu bar and its commands, refer to your Excel documentation.

PRINTING CHARTS AS SEPARATE ITEMS

You can print your charts as part of the worksheets they're placed on, or you can print them as separate items.

When you want to print a chart as part of a worksheet, be sure the specific print area or range, if you've selected one, includes your chart.

To print your chart as a separate item, place your mouse pointer on the chart and double-click the left mouse button. Excel displays your chart in its own window. With the chart window active, choose the File menu's Print command to initiate the printing process.

LOOKING AHEAD

This lesson has given you a brief and practical overview of Excel's excellent charting features. For more information on the topics introduced in this lesson, refer to the following listings in the Reference section of this book.

Charting Features

Grouping Graphic Objects

Inserting Objects in Documents

Object Movement to Back and Front

Object Property Control

Tool Bar Control

Lesson 6 shows you some basic macro techniques for automating repetitive worksheet tasks.

Automating Your Work with Macros

INTRODUCING

Creating simple macros

Using the Record and Run commands

Some macro recording tips

Working with macro sheets

Excel lets you create separate programs called macros to automate simple, repetitive sequences of keystrokes, or to use powerful applications like point-of-sale accounting and inventory management.

RECORDING AND RUNNING MACROS

This lesson shows you how to create a simple macro with the Record command and how to put it to work with the Run command. If you haven't already done so, start Excel and display a blank worksheet.

Excel's Record command creates macros by recording keystrokes and other actions. You can also write your own macros from scratch by entering macro functions, or commands, directly into a macro sheet. If you want to create a complex macro not easily constructed with the recorder, this approach can be indispensable.

THE RECORD COMMAND

The easiest way to create a macro is by using the Record command to record the actions you want to automate. Let's create a macro to enter the label *International Amalgamated, Incorporated*. While you could manually type this label each time you wanted it entered, your macro automates the process for you.

To begin, move the cell selector to the empty cell where you want the label entered. Choose the Record command from the Macro menu to display the dialog box shown in Figure 6.1.

Enter a name for your macro in the Name text box. You can use any combination of letters and numbers to name your macro, but you can't use spaces. You can also enter a shortcut key that works with the Ctrl key to start your macro. Excel assigns letters in alphabetical order as default shortcut keys.

Excel stores your macros like regular worksheet files with the file extension .XLM. When you record a macro, the Store Macro In option buttons let you choose to store your macro in the GLOBAL.XLM file or in a separate new file you can save, rename, and open much like you would a regular worksheet file. If you want your macro available at all times, mark the Global Macro Sheet button.

FIGURE 6.1:

The Record Macro dialog box

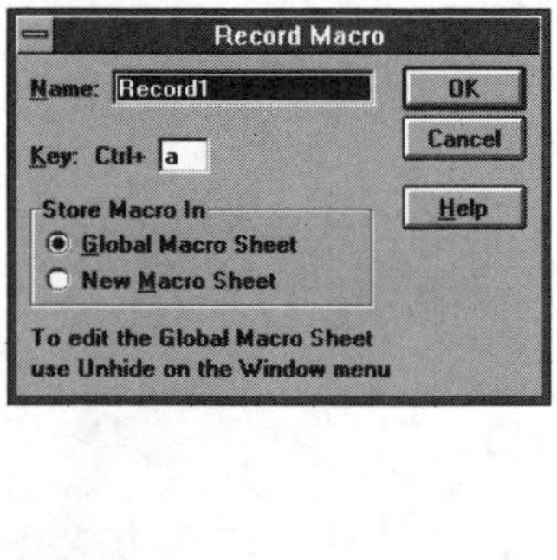

> **Record Macro**
>
> Name: Record1
>
> Key: Ctrl+ a
>
> OK
> Cancel
> Help
>
> Store Macro In
> ● Global Macro Sheet
> ○ New Macro Sheet
>
> To edit the Global Macro Sheet use Unhide on the Window menu

Complete the Record Macro dialog box and select OK to start the recorder. When Excel displays the word "Recording" on the status bar, type **International Amalgamated, Incorporated** and then press ↵. Figure 6.2 shows your worksheet with the label entered in cell A1.

Select the Stop Recorder command from the Macro menu to complete the process.

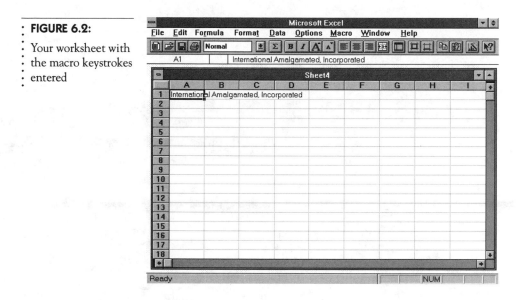

FIGURE 6.2:

Your worksheet with the macro keystrokes entered

THE RUN COMMAND

To run your macro, move the cell selector to an empty cell such as C3, and press the shortcut key combination you assigned your macro. Excel automatically enters the label you recorded as shown in Figure 6.3.

You can also run your macro by selecting the Run command from the Macro menu. Excel displays the dialog box shown in Figure 6.4.

The Run list box shows the shortcut key, file name followed by an exclamation point, and the names of each of your macros. Figure 6.4 shows the letter "n" as the shortcut key and the word "namer" as the macro name. The Reference box shows the macro selected in the Run list box. Use the OK command button to run your selected macro.

To verify the operation of your macros, use the Step command button to display the Single Step dialog box. This feature lets you step through a selected macro action by action.

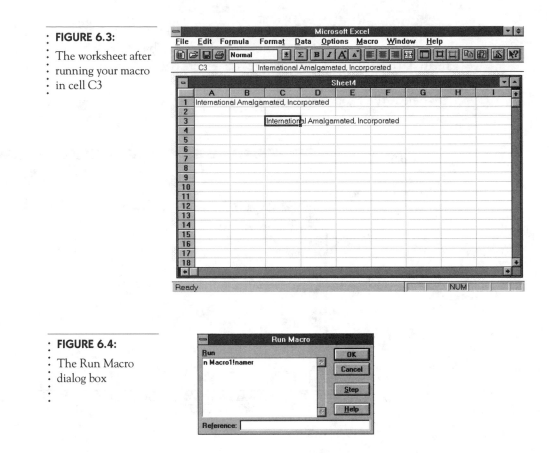

FIGURE 6.3:

The worksheet after running your macro in cell C3

FIGURE 6.4:

The Run Macro dialog box

MACRO RECORDER TIPS

The Record command also lets you record macros composed of other actions such as menu command choices, cell selector and cursor movements, and the selection of worksheet ranges. As you record more complex sequences, the following factors and features come into play.

Commands You Can't Record The macro recorder doesn't accept commands from the application window's control menu or record commands you choose from the Macro menu. It also doesn't record your choices when you select the Cancel button on a dialog box.

Recording Relative Cell References By default, Excel assumes recorded cell selector movements should be absolute. When you record selector movement from one cell to another, Excel treats the action as if you used the Formula menu's Goto command. If you want to record relative cell selector movements, or the specific methods and steps you used to get from one cell to another, choose the Relative Reference command from the Macro menu. To return to the default setting, choose the Absolute Reference command.

Pausing the Recorder To temporarily suspend your recording session, choose the Macro menu's Stop Recorder command. To start recording again, use the Start Recorder command.

WORKING WITH MACRO SHEETS

Macro sheets use the same techniques for printing, saving, and retrieving as regular worksheets. To retrieve a macro sheet file, use the Open command on the File menu. Remember, macro sheet files use an .XLM extension.

If you want to display a blank macro sheet so you can write a macro from scratch, choose the File menu's New command and select the Macro Sheet option from the dialog box.

To print a macro sheet, make its window active by selecting the document from the Window menu, and then choose the File menu's Print command. If you want to print a selected area of your macro sheet, use the Set Print Area command on the Options menu.

Excel hides the GLOBAL.XLM macro sheet document. To unhide it so you can make it active and print the macros you've stored in it, use the Window menu's Unhide command.

To save a macro sheet, first make its window active, and then use the Save or Save As command on the File menu. Use the Save As command the first time you save your macro sheet so you can name it and specify its disk and directory location. Use the Save command for subsequent saves. Excel adds the .XLM file extension automatically.

For more information on saving, retrieving, and printing, see the appropriate headings in Lessons 1, 2, and 4.

LOOKING AHEAD

This lesson has introduced you to the quickest and most convenient way to create simple macros. For more information on the subjects covered in this lesson, consult the following topics in the Reference section of this book.

Add-ins Options

Grouping Worksheets and Macro Sheets

Macro Recording and Running

Macro Set Recorder

Macro Start and Stop Recorder

Macro Relative and Absolute Recording

Macro Resume Recording

Macros Assigned to Objects

The seventh and final lesson conveys some useful information on organizing your work with Excel's database capabilities.

ORGANIZING INFORMATION WITH DATABASES

INTRODUCING

Creating databases in Excel

Editing and sorting your databases

Finding and extracting records

Printing, saving, and retrieving databases

Databases are an excellent framework for storing, identifying, and accessing quantities of information. While specialized database applications are capable of handling large volumes of complicated data, Excel's spreadsheet format and Data menu commands provide you with the basic tools for creating simple databases within the context of the program.

CREATING DATABASES

Databases are collections of related information. Individual entries are called records, and each record contains one or more fields to hold data. This lesson shows you how to create and work with a simple telephone directory database using Excel. If you haven't already done so, start Excel and display a blank worksheet.

DEFINING YOUR DATABASE

To begin defining your database, enter the field names in the first row of your worksheet as shown in Figure 7.1. Each field name must be unique. Use the Save As command on the File menu to save and name your worksheet PHONES.XLS.

To tell Excel you're creating a database, select a range that includes the row with your field names and at least one empty row below, and then choose the Set database command from the Data menu. Your database is now defined and ready to receive data.

ENTERING DATA

Choose the Form command from the Data menu to display the dialog box shown in Figure 7.2. Excel uses your database field names to label the text boxes.

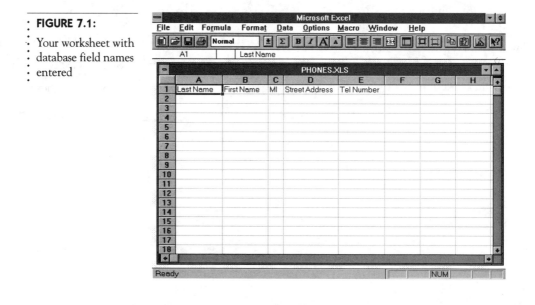

FIGURE 7.1:

Your worksheet with database field names entered

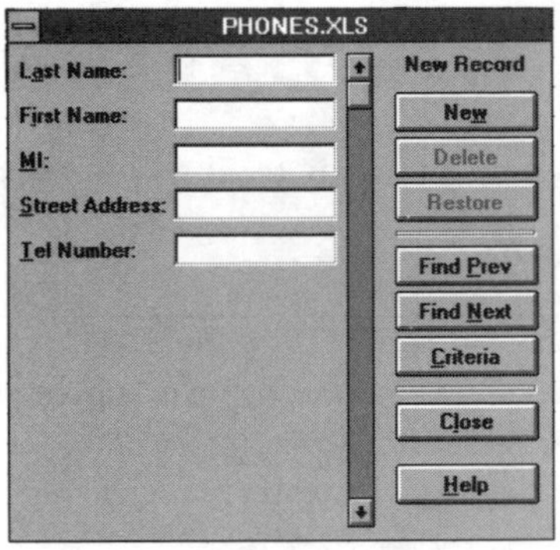

FIGURE 7.2:

Your customized data entry dialog box

To enter information into the fields of your database record, move the selection cursor to the appropriate text box and type in your data. When you've completed the record in each dialog box, press ↵. Excel enters the record into the next row of your worksheet range.

To add additional records, as shown in Figure 7.3, repeat this process. When all your records are entered, select the Close button.

TIP

To clear all the entries in a dialog box so you can enter a corrected or new record, select the New command button.

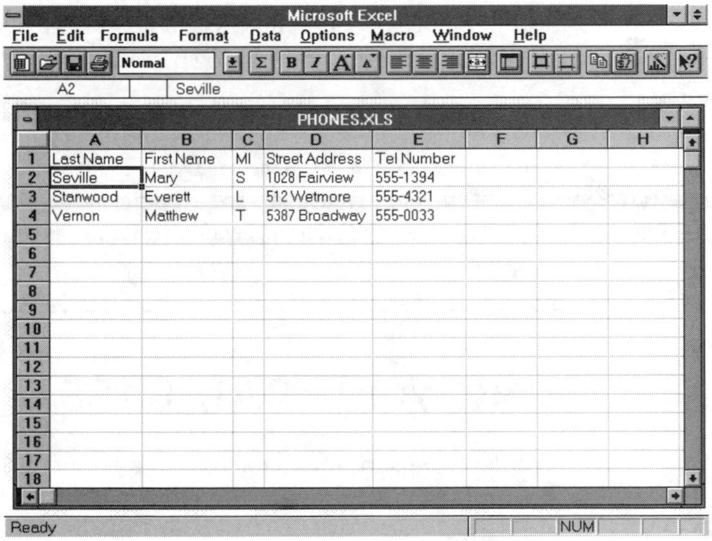

FIGURE 7.3:

Your completed PHONES.XLS database

WORKING WITH DATABASES

Excel provides a set of handy tools that let you easily update, retrieve, and organize your databases.

Microsoft Excel 4 comes with a separate application called Q+E that lets you access and update dBASE files, SQL Server files, Oracle files, and even Microsoft Excel files if they have a defined database. For more information on this application, refer to your Q+E User Guide.

EDITING DATABASE RECORDS

You can edit your database the same way you edit any other worksheet, or you can use the Form command. When you choose the Form command from the Data menu, Excel displays a dialog box like the one shown in Figure 7.2.

Display your records in the text boxes by using the PageUp and PageDn keys, the Up and Down arrow keys, the mouse and the scroll bar, or the Find Prev and Find Next command buttons. When the record you want to edit is displayed, make your changes by entering the correct data, and then display another database record or select the Close button to complete the process.

To undo your edits, select the Restore command button before displaying another record or using the Close button. To permanently delete a record, first find and display it on the Form dialog box, and then select the Delete command button.

You can also use the Data menu's Delete command to delete multiple records that match certain criteria. Before using the Delete command, you must define your search criteria. See the section on finding and extracting records in this lesson for more information on this process.

SORTING YOUR DATABASE

Excel lets you sort your databases in a variety of ways to make them easier to use. To begin, select all the database records you wish to sort. Do not select the database field names.

To select database records with your mouse, point to the first field of the first record and, holding down the left mouse button, drag the mouse pointer to the last field in the last record.

When you've selected the records you want to sort, choose the Sort command from the Data menu. Excel displays the dialog box shown in Figure 7.4.

If you've entered your records in rows, mark the Rows option button. To specify the 1st key or criteria you want used in sorting your records, enter the cell address of the field that describes the key as an absolute reference. To sort your PHONES.XLS database by last names, enter **A2** in the 1st Key box. Choose the Ascending or Descending option button as desired.

Use the 2nd and 3rd key settings to control sorting of records with identical 1st or 2nd keys. In our directory example, you could specify the first name field as a 2nd key to accommodate entries with the same last name. When your dialog box is complete, select OK to begin the sorting process.

If you make a mistake sorting your database, use the Edit menu's Undo command to reverse the operation. Remember, the Undo command only affects the last action you performed.

FIGURE 7.4:

The Sort dialog box

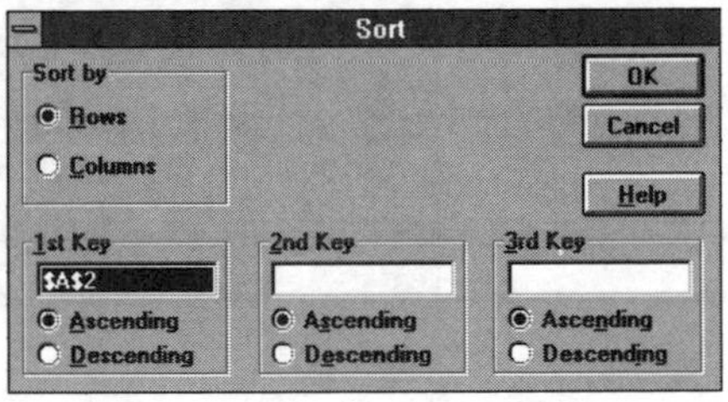

FINDING AND EXTRACTING RECORDS

FINDING AND EXTRACTING RECORDS

With large databases, it can be difficult to locate a specific record or group of records with common characteristics. Excel provides a simple way to search or query your database using the Form command's dialog box, and a more sophisticated method using specified search criteria and the Data menu's Find command.

QUERYING YOUR DATABASE

To query your database, display the Form command's dialog box and select the Criteria command button. Excel displays the Criteria dialog box shown in Figure 7.5.

If you want to find a database record with the last name Seville, enter **Seville** in the Last Name text box, and then select the Find Next or Find Prev command buttons to search your database. If Excel finds a record that matches your criteria, it displays the record in the Form dialog box.

To query your database for numeric values, the numeric criterion you enter must be preceded by a comparison operator. Excel accepts comparison operators such as = for equal to, > for greater than, < for less than, <> for not equal to, >= for greater than or equal to, and <= for less than or equal to. You would enter >=1000 if you want Excel to search for values greater than or equal to 1000.

To return to the Standard Form dialog box to enter, edit or delete your database records, select the Form button on the Criteria dialog box.

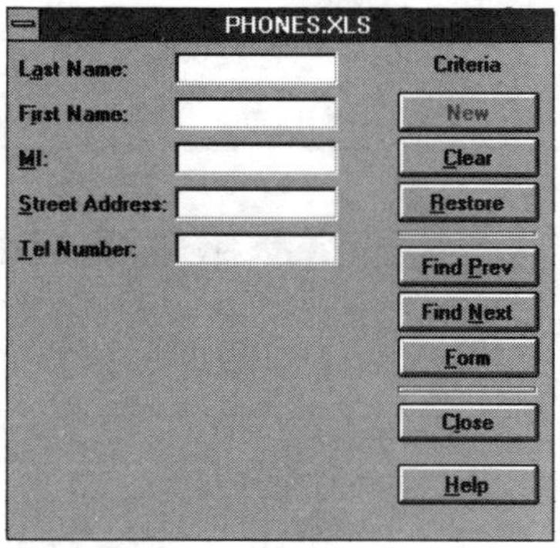

FIGURE 7.5:

The Criteria
dialog box

PHONES.XLS	
Last Name:	Criteria
First Name:	New
MI:	Clear
Street Address:	Restore
Tel Number:	
	Find Prev
	Find Next
	Form
	Close
	Help

THE FIND COMMAND

To locate a record using the Find command, you must first enter your search criterion in a worksheet range, with the field name entered in one cell, and the criterion value entered in the cell directly below. If you were looking for the telephone number of someone name Stanwood, you would enter **Last Name**, which is the field name, in the first cell, and then the criterion value **Stanwood** in the cell directly below.

Next, identify the worksheet range holding your search criterion, by selecting the range, and then choosing the Set Criteria command from the Data menu. Choose the Find command from the Data menu to begin the search operation.

When Excel locates a record, it moves the cell selector to the first cell in the record. You can press ⏎ to move between fields and find the specific entry you're seeking. Choose the Repeat command on the Edit menu to continue the search operation, and use the Exit Find command on the Data menu to stop the process.

To specify multiple search criteria, simply enter additional values in the cells below the field name cell and use the cells in adjacent columns to enter additional field names. Select the entire range that defines your multiple search criteria, choose the Set Criteria command, and then the Find command to start the operation.

The Extract Command

The Data menu's Extract command lets you extract records of a particular type and regroup them in another location on the same database worksheet. First, use the method you learned earlier to specify a search criterion for the records you want extracted. Next, tell Excel where to place your extracted records by copying and pasting the row with your database field names to a new location on your worksheet.

Select the range containing your copied and pasted field names, and then choose the Set Extract command from the Data menu. When you choose the Extract command from the Data menu, Excel copies all the records that match your extraction criterion to the rows below the selected field name row.

Excel may paste extracted records over existing data. If the cells containing your selection criteria are below your selected field name row, all the records in your database may be extracted if the criterion cells are pasted over. You can limit the scope of your operation by including a specific number of empty rows below the field name row in your selected range.

PRINTING, SAVING, AND RETRIEVING

Since databases are essentially worksheets, you can use the same techniques to print, save, and retrieve them. Databases even use the same .XLS file extension.

To print a database, use the File menu's Print command. You can also use the Option menu's Set Print Area command to designate a specific worksheet range for printing.

To save a database, use the File menu's Save As and Save commands. The Save As command lets you name your database and specify its disk location. Use the Save command for subsequent saves.

To retrieve a database, use the File menu's Open command. Locate and identify your database file on the File Open dialog box, and select OK to complete the process.

LOOKING AHEAD

This lesson has given you a fast yet comprehensive look at creating and working with Excel databases. For more information on the topics introduced in this lesson, refer to the following listings in the Reference section of this book.

Deleting Database Records

Extracting Database Records

Finding Database Records

Form for Data Entry

Q+E Application

Setting Criteria for Database Search

Setting Database Ranges

Setting Extraction Ranges

Sorting Worksheet Data

If you've completed each of the lessons in the Tutorial section of this book, you should now possess the basic skills necessary to work with Excel on a practical level. Refer to the Reference section as you broaden your understanding of the powerful features of this program.

PART TWO

REFERENCE

ADD-INS OPTIONS

MENU PATH Options ➤ Add-ins

The Add-ins command lets you specify which add-in macro files Excel should open whenever it starts. By opening the add-in macro files as part of starting Excel, you can use the add-in macros any time you want.

By default, Excel opens several add-in macros, including macros to run the Solver command, the Scenario Manager command, and the Analysis Tools command. There are also more than a dozen other add-in macros that come with Excel.

NOTE Refer to your Microsoft Excel User Guide for more information.

ALIGNING VALUES AND LABELS

MENU PATH Format ➤ Alignment

SHORTCUTS Left align tool, Center align tool, Right align tool, Center across tool

The Alignment command controls how values and labels are vertically and horizontally aligned in cells as well as how they are oriented. You can also align labels and values with the tools provided on the Excel tool bar. To use the Alignment command, first select the worksheet range that you want to align, and then follow these steps:

1. Choose the Alignment command from either the Format or Shortcuts menu to display the Alignment dialog box.

2. Use the Horizontal option buttons (General, Left, Center, Right, Fill, Justify, and Center across) to control horizontal alignment within cells.

- General, the default setting, causes values to be right-justified and labels to be left-justified.

- Left causes both values and labels to be left-justified.

- Center causes both values and labels to be centered in cells.

- Right causes both values and labels to be right-justified.

- Fill repeats a label or value as many times as it will fit in a cell.

- Justify both left and right-justified text within a cell and automatically resizes the row containing the selected cell to accommodate the justified text within the cell.

- Center across centers a label or value across the width of the selected range.

3. Use the Vertical option buttons (Top, Center, and Bottom) to vertically align labels and values in cells.

- Top causes labels and values to be top-justified so they are positioned flush against the top edge of the cell.

- Center causes labels and values to be centered between the top and bottom edges of the cell.

- Bottom causes labels and values to be bottom-justified so they are positioned flush against the bottom edge of the cell.

4. The Wrap Text check box justifies text in a cell and also automatically adjusts row height to accomodate the wrapped text within the cell.

5. The Orientation command buttons rotate labels and values as shown.

NOTE You may need to adjust the height of rows in the selected range so the rotated text can be read in the worksheet.

ANALYSIS TOOLS FOR SPECIAL USES

MENU PATH Options ➤ Analysis Tools

The Options menu's Analysis Tools command displays a list of the special engineering, financial, and statistical tools provided in the Analysis Toolpack Add-in. To

use one of these tools, choose the Analysis Tools command, select the tool you want from the list Excel displays, and then respond to Excel's prompts.

NOTE The Analysis Toolpack includes two engineering tools (Fourier Analysis and Sampling) and 17 other tools for making financial, and statistical calculations.

ARRANGING WINDOW SIZE AND POSITION

MENU PATH Window ➤ Arrange

The Window menu's Arrange command resizes and moves the open document windows so they can all be viewed as tiles in the Excel application window. The Arrange command also lets you specify whether the window showing a copy of a document should be synchronized to move as you scroll the window showing the original document.

NOTE If you've minimized all the document windows, Excel replaces the Arrange command with the Arrange Icons command. The Arrange Icons command neatly arranges the document window icons along the bottom edge of the Excel application window.

AUTOMATIC FORMATTING

MENU PATH Format ➤ AutoFormat

SHORTCUT AutoFormat tool

The Format menu's AutoFormat command allows you to simultaneously perform a series of formatting tasks such as value formatting, label and value alignment, font style changes, and so forth. To use the AutoFormat feature, follow these steps:

1. Select the worksheet range you want to format.
2. Choose the AutoFormat command to display the AutoFormat dialog box.

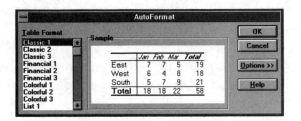

3. From the Table Format list box, select one of the sets of formatting rules. Refer to the Sample box to see how a table formatted according to the selected set of table formatting rules appears.

NOTE To apply your selected AutoFormat style to another range on your worksheet, use the AutoFormat tool on the tool bar.

SEE ALSO Formatting Numbers, Aligning Values and Labels, Font Styles, Bordering and Shading Cells and Ranges, Patterns and Cell Shading

BORDERING AND SHADING CELLS AND RANGES

MENU PATH Format ➤ Border

SHORTCUTS Draw box tool, Draw line tool

The Border command lets you create borders around cells and worksheet ranges, and also shade cells and draw lines. To use the command, follow these steps:

1. Select the worksheet range you want to draw on or shade.

2. Choose the Border command from either the Format menu or the Shortcuts menu to display the Border dialog box.

3. To tell Excel where to draw a line, use the Border option buttons.

   ◆ Mark the Outline button to draw a line around the outside edge of the selected worksheet range.

   ◆ Mark the Left, Right, Top, or Bottom buttons to draw a line along a specific edge of the selected range.

4. To shade the cells in the selected range, mark the Shade check box.

5. To describe the type of line you want drawn, use the Style buttons.

6. To choose a color other than black, activate the Color drop down list box.

SEE ALSO Patterns and Cell Shading

CALCULATING WORKSHEETS

MENU PATH Options ➤ Calculation

SHORTCUT F9

The Options menu's Calculation command lets you control whether worksheet recalculation is automatically initiated by Excel or manually initiated by the user. You can also use the Calculation command to control more esoteric aspects of worksheet calculation such as how many times circular references are iteratively recalculated and how linked formulas are recalculated.

NOTE To manually initiate recalculation, press F9 or select the Calc Now or Calc Doc buttons on the Calculation dialog box.

CELL PROTECTION

MENU PATH Format ➤ Cell Protection

The Cell Protection command works with the Options menu's Protect Document command to let you identify cells that can't be modified and can't have their contents viewed on the formula bar once document protection has been activated. To use the Cell Protection command, follow these steps:

1. Select the worksheet range containing the cells you want to protect.

2. Choose the Cell Protection command from the Format menu to display the Cell Protection dialog box.

3. To protect cells in the selected worksheet range from having their contents modified once the Protect Document command is chosen, mark the Locked check box.

4. To prevent cells in the selected worksheet range from having their con-tents viewed on the formula bar once the Protect Document command is chosen, mark the Hidden check box.

SEE ALSO Protecting Documents

CHARTING FEATURES

SHORTCUT ChartWizard tool

Excel provides two methods for creating charts. Lesson 5 in this book shows you how to use the ChartWizard, which is the easiest method of chart creation.

The Chart menu commands appear whenever the active document window dis-plays a chart. You can use the Chart menu commands to create charts from scratch.

NOTE For more information on the Chart menu commands, refer to your Microsoft Excel User Guide.

CLEARING UNWANTED DATA

MENU PATH Edit ➤ Clear

The Clear command erases the contents, formats, or notes of selected cells. To use the Clear command, follow these steps:

1. Choose the Clear command from the Edit or Shortcuts menu to display the Clear dialog box.

2. Mark the Formulas button to erase cell contents, Formats to erase cell for-mats, Notes to erase cell notes, or All to erase everything.

CLOSING FILES

MENU PATH File ➤ Close

SHORTCUTS Ctrl-F4 (closes the active document window), Shift-F4 (closes all document windows)

The File menu's Close command closes the active document window. If the active window hasn't been saved, Excel asks if you want to save the file.

NOTE To close all the document windows, press the Shift key and the Shortcut key F4. When you press the Shift key, Excel also changes the Close command on the File menu to the Close All command.

SEE ALSO Saving Files

COLOR PALETTE FOR DOCUMENT WINDOWS

MENU PATH Options ➤ Color Palette

The Option menu's Color Palette command lets you choose a set of colors for your Excel document windows. When you choose this command, Excel displays the Color Palette dialog box.

To change one of the colors, double-click on the color button, and when Excel displays the Color Picker dialog box, choose the new color you want.

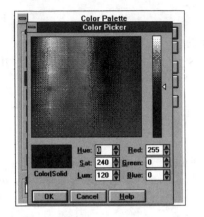

You can indicate a color by picking it from the Color Picker's color spectrum chart (specifying its hue, saturation, and luminescence) or by specifying the amount of red, green, or blue in the color.

COLUMN WIDTH CHANGES

MENU PATH Format ➤ Column Width

The Column Width command lets you increase, decrease, or even hide columns by changing their width to zero. To use the Column Width command, follow these steps:

1. Select the column or columns you want to change.

2. Choose the Column Width command from the Format menu to display the Column Width dialog box.

3. Enter the desired width in characters in the Column Width text box. To reset the column width to the 8.43 default dimension, mark the Use Standard Width check box. To adjust the column width to hold the widest label or value, select the Best Fit command button. To hide a column, select the Hide command button.

NOTE A hidden column is shown as a bold line between letters on the column border. To unhide a column, select the range of columns that includes the column both to the left and right of the hidden column. Choose the Column Width command to display the Column Width dialog box, and then select the Unhide command button.

CONSOLIDATING DATA

MENU PATH Data ➤ Consolidate

The Data menu's Consolidate command lets you combine and summarize data from more than one range and more than one worksheet into a single range on a single worksheet.

NOTE For more information on the Consolidate command, refer to your Microsoft Excel User Guide.

COPYING DATA TO THE CLIPBOARD

MENU PATH Edit ➤ Copy

SHORTCUTS Ctrl-C, Copy tool

The Copy command duplicates the data in a selected worksheet range and temporarily stores it in the Windows clipboard. The Copy command is usually used in combination with the Paste command to duplicate data in other locations. To use the Copy command, first select the worksheet range containing the data you want to duplicate, and then choose the Copy command from the Edit menu or the Shortcuts menu.

SEE ALSO Cutting Selected Worksheet Data, Pasting Data from the Clipboard

CUTTING SELECTED WORKSHEET DATA

MENU PATH Edit ➤ Cut

SHORTCUTS Ctrl-X, Shift-Delete

The Cut command removes data in a selected worksheet range and stores it temporarily in the Windows clipboard. The Cut command is usually used in combination with the Edit menu's Paste command to remove data and place it in another location. First select the worksheet range you want to remove, and then choose the Cut command from either the Edit or Shortcuts menu.

SEE ALSO Copying Data to the Clipboard, Pasting Data from the Clipboard

DELETING COLUMNS AND ROWS

MENU PATH Edit ➤ Delete

SHORTCUT Ctrl-hyphen

The Delete command lets you delete selected cells or entire columns and rows. Choose the Delete command from either the Edit menu or the Shortcuts menu to display the Delete dialog box. Mark the appropriate option buttons and then select OK.

The Shift Cells Left button moves the cells on the right of the deleted cells to the left. The Shift Cells Up button moves the cells below the deleted cells up. You can also delete the entire row or column, in which there are selected cells, by marking the Entire Row or Entire Column buttons.

NOTE You can also delete entire rows or columns by selecting the row number or column letter in the worksheet border, and then choosing the Delete command.

DELETING DATABASE RECORDS

MENU PATH Data ➤ Delete

The Data menu's Delete command removes database records that match designated search criteria. The records must be within a database you've defined using the Set Database command, and the search criteria must have already been specified using the Set Criteria command.

NOTE See Lesson 7 in this book for a detailed tutorial on defining search criteria and deleting database records.

SEE ALSO Setting Database Ranges, Setting Criteria for Database Search

DELETING FILES

MENU PATH File ➤ Delete

The File menu's Delete command erases files stored on disk. To use the File Delete command, follow these steps:

1. Choose the Delete command from the File menu to display the Delete Document dialog box.

2. Move the selection cursor to the Drives list box, and specify the disk where the file you want is stored.

3. Move the selection cursor to the Directories list box, and specify in which directory the file is stored.

4. Move the selection cursor to the File Name text box and enter the file name, or select the file from the File Name list box.

5. Select OK to complete the process.

DISPLAYING DOCUMENT WINDOWS

MENU PATH Options ➤ Display

The Display command lets you control how Excel displays document windows. When you choose this command, Excel displays the Display Options dialog box.

Use the Cells check boxes to specify whether cells should show formulas (rather than formula results), gridlines, row and column headings, calculated zero values, outline symbols, and automatic page breaks. The Objects buttons specify whether Excel should display embedded objects, show placeholders to identify the object's location, or hide all objects. The Gridline & Heading Color list allows you to specify color for gridlines, row numbers, and column letters.

SEE ALSO Color Palette for Document Windows

DRAWING FEATURES

SHORTCUTS Draw box tool, Draw line tool, Drawing tool bar tools

The Draw box and Draw line tools, which are described in Lesson 3, let you draw borders around or lines under worksheet ranges. You can also use the tools on the Drawing tool bar to create lines and shapes.

To display the Drawing tool bar, use the Options menu's Toolbar command. To draw a line or shape using a Drawing tool, select a tool with an icon like the line or shape you want to draw.

SEE ALSO Bordering and Shading Cells and Ranges, Inserting Objects in Documents, Grouping Graphic Objects, Object Movement Back to Front, Object Property Control, Tool Bar Control

EXITING EXCEL

MENU PATH File ➤ Exit

SHORTCUT Alt-F4

The Exit command stops the Excel Application program. This command is equivalent to closing the Excel application window by choosing the Close command from the Application window's control menu. If you haven't saved the open worksheet files since the last changes were made, Excel prompts you to save them before exiting.

SEE ALSO Saving Files

EXTRACTING DATABASE RECORDS

MENU PATH Data ➤ Extract

The Extract command copies database records that match designated search criteria. The database records must be within a database you've defined using the Set Database command, and the search criteria must have already been specified using the Set Criteria command. The range to which the copied records are to be pasted must also have been specified using the Set Extract command.

NOTE Lesson 7 in this book has a detailed tutorial on this process.

SEE ALSO Setting Database Ranges, Setting Extraction Ranges, Setting Criteria for Database Search

E

FILLING CELL DATA INTO SELECTED RANGES

MENU PATH Edit ➤ Fill Right/Fill Down

SHORTCUTS Ctrl-R, Ctrl-D

The Fill Right and Fill Down commands copy labels, values, or formulas, and then fill the cells in a selected range with the copied data. The Fill Left and Fill Up commands replace Fill Right and Fill Down on the Edit menu when you press the Shift key.

To use the Fill commands, first select the worksheet range that includes the data you want copied and the cells you want to fill. Choose the Fill Right or Fill Down command, or press Shift and choose Fill Left or Fill Up to complete the process.

FINDING CELL DATA

MENU PATH Formula ➤ Find

SHORTCUT Shift-F5

The Find command lets you search through worksheets and macro sheets for specific labels, values, formulas, or formula results. To use the Find command, follow these steps:

1. Select the worksheet range you want to search. Excel searches your entire worksheet if you don't select a specific range.

2. Choose the Find command from the Formula menu to display the Find dialog box.

3. Enter the label, value, formula, or formula result you want to find in the Find What text box.

4. Use the Look In option buttons to tell Excel where to search.

5. Use the Look At option buttons to tell Excel whether it must find whole, or exact matches, or can partly match a cell's contents.

6. Use the Look By option buttons to specify a search by row or column.

7. The Match Case check box tells Excel to exactly match the case of the Find What entry.

NOTE If Excel finds a label, value, formula, or formula result that matches the search description you entered using the Find dialog box, it moves the cell selector to that cell. To repeat the search, press the Find function key, F7.

SEE ALSO Replacing Cell Data, Selecting Special Cell Characteristics

FINDING DATABASE RECORDS

MENU PATH Data ➤ Find

The Find command moves the cell selector to database records that match designated search criteria. The database records must be within a database you've defined using the Set Database command, and the search criteria must have already been specified using the Set Criteria command.

NOTES After you've selected the Find command, scrolling moves the cell selector only to database records that match the search criteria. To turn off the Find mode, choose the Data menu's Exit Find command, which replaces the Find command when Find is activated.

See Lesson 7 in this book for a tutorial on using the Find command.

SEE ALSO Setting Database Ranges, Setting Criteria for Database Search

FONT STYLES

MENU PATH Format ➤ Font

SHORTCUTS Bold tool, Italic tool, Next size larger tool, Next size smaller tool

The Font command lets you change the default font style from 10 point Helvetica. To use the Font command, follow these steps:

1. Select the range where you want to change the font style, and then choose the Font command from either the Format menu or the Shortcuts menu to display the Font dialog box.

2. Select the font name from the Fonts list box.

3. Select the desired style (Regular, Italic, Bold, etc.) from the Font Style list box.

4. Change the font point size with the Size list box.

5. The Strikeout check box draws a line through the characters in the selected range.

6. The Underline check box underlines the selected characters.

7. To use a color other than black, activate the Color list and choose the desired color.

NOTE The Sample text box displays an example of the current font selection. The Normal Font check box returns the selections to the default settings.

FORM FOR DATA ENTRY

MENU PATH Data ➤ Form

The Form command creates a dialog box for entering data into a database and editing database information. The dialog box includes text boxes for each of the database fields, as well as several command buttons that make data entry easier.

To use the command, you need to have previously defined a database using the Data menu's Set Database command.

NOTE Refer to Lesson 7 for a tutorial on creating databases and using the form command.

SEE ALSO Setting Database Ranges

FORMATTING NUMBERS

MENU PATH Format ➤ Number

The Number command formats values in the selected worksheet range. Formatted values use punctuation such as commas, percent symbols, parenthesis marks, and dollar signs to make values easier to read. To use the Number command, select the worksheet range you want to format, and then follow these steps:

1. Choose the Number command from either the Format or the Shortcuts menu to display the Number Format dialog box.

Number Format	
Category	**Format Codes**
All	General
Number	0
Currency	0.00
Date	#,##0
Time	#,##0.00
Percentage	$#,##0_);($#,##0)
Fraction	$#,##0_);[Red]($#,##0)
Scientific	$#,##0.00_);($#,##0.00)

Buttons: OK, Cancel, Delete, Help

Code: General

Sample:

2. Select a format category and style from the Category and Format Codes list boxes.

3. Select OK to complete the process.

NOTE Refer to the Sample text box at the bottom of the dialog box to view an example of your format code selection.

FREEZING PANES ON SPLIT DOCUMENT WINDOWS

MENU PATH Window ➤ Freeze Panes

The Freeze Panes command lets you freeze the top pane, the left pane, or both the top and left panes of a split window so the panes can't be scrolled.

NOTE The Unfreeze Panes command replaces the Freeze Panes command when it has been activated.

SEE ALSO Splitting Windows into Panes

F

GOTO COMMAND

MENU PATH Formula ➤ Goto

SHORTCUT F5

The Goto command moves the cell selector to a specified cell without scrolling through your worksheet. The Goto command can also move the cell selector to the upper left corner of a named range.

Choose the Goto command from the Formula menu or press F5 to display the Goto dialog box.

Enter the address of the cell you want to go to in the Reference text box. To move the cell selector to the upper-left corner of a named range, select the range from the Goto list box.

NOTE To have items listed in the Goto list box, you must first create named ranges on your worksheet. Refer to Lesson 2 for a tutorial on naming and working with ranges.

SEE ALSO Naming Ranges

GROUPING GRAPHIC OBJECTS

MENU PATH Format ➤ Group

The Group command lets you form one graphic object from a group of other selected graphic objects. The Group command makes it easier to move and re-size more than one object at a time.

To use the Group command, first select each of the graphic objects to be included in the new group by holding down the Ctrl key and then clicking on each of the objects. Choose the Group command to complete the process.

NOTE The Ungroup command is displayed on the Format menu when a selected object was created using the Group command.

SEE ALSO Drawing Features, Inserting Objects in Documents, Object Movement Back to Front, Object Property Control

GROUPING WORKSHEETS AND MACROSHEETS

MENU PATH Options ➤ Group Edit

The Group Edit command lets you group worksheets and macro sheets so subsequent commands and changes applied to one worksheet effect the entire group.

NOTE For more information, refer to your Microsoft Excel User Guide.

HELP FOR LOTUS 1-2-3 USERS

MENU PATH Help ➤ Lotus 1-2-3

The Lotus 1-2-3 Help command makes it easier for former Lotus 1-2-3 users to use Excel. The Lotus 1-2-3 Help command lets you choose a Lotus 1-2-3 command, such as Worksheet Insert Row, and then view the equivalent Excel command performed step-by-step.

SEE ALSO Learning Microsoft Excel

HELP FOR MICROSOFT MULTIPLAN USERS

MENU PATH Help ➤ Multiplan Help

The Multiplan Help command makes it easier for former Microsoft Multiplan users to begin using Excel. When you choose a Multiplan command, the equivalent Excel command is executed step by step so you can see how Excel works.

SEE ALSO Learning Microsoft Excel

HELP ON EXCEL

MENU PATH Help ➤ Contents/Search

The Help menu's Contents command starts the Windows Help application and displays a list of general help topics.

To see specific listings within a category, click on the topic name. To get help information on a specific topic, click on it.

The Search command starts the Windows Help application and displays the Search dialog box.

Enter the topic you want to search for in the text box, and then select the general and specific categories Excel displays in the list boxes.

NOTES Help topics are identified with a special color, usually green, on the Help application windows, and when you point to a help topic in text, Windows changes the mouse pointer to a hand.

You can also choose the Search command by selecting the Search button on the Help Contents window.

SEE ALSO Help for Lotus 1-2-3 Users, Help for Microsoft Multiplan Users

HIDING DOCUMENT WINDOWS

MENU PATH Window ➤ Hide

The Hide command hides the active document so it is not visible in the application window. This command is usually employed to hide windows that need to be open but that you don't need to display, such as macro sheets.

SEE ALSO Unhiding Document Windows

INSERTING COLUMNS AND ROWS

MENU PATH Edit ➤ Insert

SHORTCUT Ctrl-Shift-+

The Insert command lets you insert columns and rows in a worksheet. To insert entire rows or columns, select the row number above where you want a new row inserted or the column letter to the left of where you want a new column inserted. To insert cells in rows or columns, select a number of cells above or to the left of where you want the same number of new cells inserted, and then choose the Insert command to display the Insert dialog box.

Use the Shift Cells Right and Shift Cells Down buttons to tell Excel how to adjust your worksheet to fit the newly inserted cells. Select OK to complete the process.

NOTE You can also insert entire rows or columns with the Entire Row or Entire Column option buttons.

INSERTING OBJECTS IN DOCUMENTS

MENU PATH Edit ➤ Insert Object

The Insert Object command lets you embed objects such as charts, worksheets, or macro sheets in open Excel documents. When you choose this command, Excel displays the Insert Object dialog box.

Simply select the object you want to insert from the Object Type list, and then select OK to complete the process.

INTRODUCING MICROSOFT EXCEL

MENU PATH Help ➤ Introducing Microsoft Excel

The Introducing Microsoft Excel command displays a screen that lets you choose one of three interactive product demonstrations.

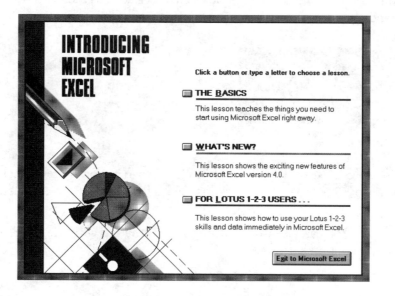

The demonstrations include an overview of the basic mechanics of the Excel program, a summary of new features for version 4.0, and an orientation for former Lotus 1-2-3 users. You can select the button to activate a demonstration, or choose the Exit to Microsoft Excel command button.

SEE ALSO Help for Lotus 1-2-3 Users, Help on Excel, Learning Microsoft Excel

JUSTIFYING TEXT

MENU PATH Format ➤ Justify

The Justify command breaks a long text label entered into a single cell into several shorter text labels that fill several cells. To use the Justify command, select a worksheet range where the upper-left corner of the range contains the cell with the long text label.

The range width should also equal the length desired for the new shortened text labels, and include as many rows as you want new labels. Choose the Justify command to complete the process.

LEARNING MICROSOFT EXCEL

MENU PATH Help ➤ Learning Microsoft Excel

The Learning Microsoft Excel command starts an interactive tutorial that teaches basic Excel skills, including explanations of how to construct worksheets, create charts, build databases, write macros, and use tool bars.

SEE ALSO Introducing Microsoft Excel

LINKING FILES

MENU PATH File ➤ Links

The Links command displays a dialog box that lists the files linked by formulas to the active file. You can also use the Links command to change the files linked to the active file, open files that are linked to the active file, and retrieve values from the files linked to the active file.

SEE ALSO Pasting Link Formulas

MACRO RECORDING AND RUNNING

MENU PATH Macro ➤ Record/Run

The Record command lets you create a macro by recording the actions you want to automate. To use the Record command, follow these steps:

1. Choose the Record command from the Macro menu to display the Record Macro dialog box.

```
┌─────────────────────────────────────┐
│ ▭          Record Macro             │
│ Name:  Record1          ▾   ┌──OK──┐ │
│                             └──────┘ │
│ Key:  Ctrl+ a               ┌Cancel┐ │
│                             └──────┘ │
│ ┌Store Macro In───────────┐ ┌─Help─┐ │
│ │ ○ Global Macro Sheet    │ └──────┘ │
│ │ ● New Macro Sheet       │          │
│ └─────────────────────────┘          │
│ To edit the Global Macro Sheet       │
│ use Unhide on the Window menu        │
└─────────────────────────────────────┘
```

2. In the Name text box, enter a name for the macro.

3. In the Key box, enter the key that when combined with the Ctrl key makes up the alternate shortcut key for running your macro.

4. Use the Store Macro In buttons to tell Excel to store your macro in the Global Macro Sheet or in a separate, New Macro Sheet.

5. Perform the actions you want your macro to perform.

6. When you are finished, choose the Stop Recorder command.

The Run command is one of the two ways you can start a macro. The other way is to type its Ctrl key combination.

To use the Run command, select it from Macro menu and display the Run Macro dialog box.

```
┌─────────────────────────────────────┐
│ ▭            Run Macro               │
│ Run                         ┌──OK──┐ │
│ d Macro1!DataEntry      ▲   └──────┘ │
│ s Macro1!Simulation         ┌Cancel┐ │
│                             └──────┘ │
│                             ┌─Step─┐ │
│                             └──────┘ │
│                         ▼   ┌─Help─┐ │
│                             └──────┘ │
│ Reference:  _____ │
└─────────────────────────────────────┘
```

Select the macro you want to run from the list box, and then select OK.

NOTES Macros in the GLOBAL.XLM macro sheet are always available. Macros in separate macro sheets are available only when those macro sheets are open.

The Step command button on the Run Macro dialog box displays the Single Step dialog box. This feature lets you run your macros step by step.

See Lesson 6 for a detailed tutorial on recording and running macros.

SEE ALSO Macro Set Recorder, Macro Start and Stop Recorder, Macro Relative and Absolute Recording, Macro Resume Recording

MACRO SET RECORDER

MENU PATH Macro ➤ Set Recorder

The Macro menu's Set Recorder command lets you specify where in the active macro sheet a macro created by the recorder should be placed.

NOTE For more information on the Macro Set Recorder command, refer to your Microsoft Excel User Guide.

MACRO START AND STOP RECORDER

MENU PATH Macro ➤ Start Recorder/Stop Recorder

The Macro menu's Start and Stop Recorder commands let you stop and then resume a macro recording session. Once a macro session is started, the Start command changes to the Stop Recorder command.

NOTE The Stop and Start Recorder commands can be very useful when there are actions you need to perform but don't want recorded in your macro.

MACRO RELATIVE AND ABSOLUTE RECORDING

MENU PATH Macro ➤ Relative Record/Absolute Record

The Relative Record and Absolute Record commands let you specify whether your macro records cell selector movements in relative or absolute terms. Excel assumes absolute references for cell selector movement and displays the Relative Record command as an option. When you choose the Relative Record command, Excel replaces it with the Absolute Record command.

NOTE When you record cell selector movements in absolute terms, they are treated as if you simply used the Formula menu's Goto command. The Relative Record command lets you record all the actions performed to move the cell selector from one place to another.

MACRO RESUME RECORDING

MENU PATH Macro ➤ Resume

The Macro menu's Resume command restarts a macro you suspended using the Pause button on the Single Step dialog box.

NOTE The Single Step dialog box is displayed when you choose the Step command button on the Run Macro dialog box. It allows you to run a macro one step at a time.

MACROS ASSIGNED TO OBJECTS

MENU PATH Macro ➤ Assign to Object

The Assign To Object command lets you connect a macro to a worksheet or macro sheet object. After the connection is made, clicking on the object starts the macro. For more information, refer to your Microsoft Excel User Guide.

NOTE To identify objects with macro connections, Excel changes the mouse pointer to a hand whenever the pointer is on a connected object.

NAMING RANGES

MENU PATH Formula ➤ Define Name

SHORTCUT Ctrl-F3

The Define Name command lets you name ranges. Once a range is named, you can use its name in commands and formulas rather than its cell address. For example, if the worksheet range A1:A50 is named COSTS, the two function formulas SUM(A1:A50) and SUM(COSTS) are equivalent. To use the Define Name command, follow these steps:

1. Select the range you want to name.

2. Choose the Define Name command from the Formula menu to display the Define Names dialog box.

3. Enter the range name in the Name text box.

4. Verify the range definition shown in the Refers to text box.

5. Choose the Add command to define additional names, and select OK to complete the process.

NOTE You can also delete selected range names using the Delete button on the Define Names dialog box.

SEE ALSO Applying Names, Creating Names, Pasting Names

APPLYING NAMES

MENU PATH Formula ➤ Apply Names

The Apply Names command lets you apply range names to range references in a selected area of a worksheet. This command can be useful when you want to update existing formulas with new range names. To use the Apply Names command, follow these steps:

1. Select the worksheet area where you want Excel to apply range names.

2. Choose the Apply Names command to display the Apply Names dialog box.

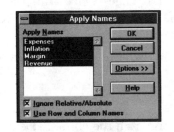

3. The names you want to apply to range references can be selected from the Apply Names list box. To select more than one range name, hold down CTRL while you click on additional names.

4. Mark or unmark the Ignore Relative/Absolute check box as desired.

5. If you unmark the Use Row and Column Names check box, select OK to complete the process.

6. If you mark the Use Row and Column Names check box, select the Options command button to display additional boxes and buttons for specifying how Excel should construct range name equivalents.

CREATING NAMES

MENU PATH Formula ➤ Create Names

SHORTCUT Ctrl-Shift-F3

The Create Names command lets you define range names using worksheet labels adjacent to the ranges you want to name. To use the Create Names command, follow these steps:

1. Select the worksheet range that includes both the labels to be used as range names and the range you want to name.

2. Choose the Create Names command from the Formula menu to display the Create Names dialog box.

```
┌─────────────────────────────────┐
│ ─           Create Names         │
│ ┌─Create Names in─┐  ┌────────┐  │
│ │ ☐ Top Row       │  │   OK   │  │
│ │ ☒ Left Column   │  └────────┘  │
│ │ ☐ Bottom Row    │  ┌────────┐  │
│ │ ☐ Right Column  │  │ Cancel │  │
│ └─────────────────┘  └────────┘  │
│                      ┌────────┐  │
│                      │  Help  │  │
│                      └────────┘  │
└─────────────────────────────────┘
```

3. Mark the appropriate check box to locate the labels you want to use as a range name.

4. Select OK to complete the process

NOTE Excel won't use values as range names. If you use the Create Names command to designate a date value as a range name, Excel converts it to a text label.

SEE ALSO Naming Ranges

PASTING NAMES

MENU PATH Formula ➤ Paste Name

SHORTCUT F3

The Paste Name command makes it easier to enter range names into formulas you're creating or editing. To use the Paste Name command, follow these steps:

1. Position the insertion point at the exact location the range name should be inserted.

2. Choose the Paste Names command from the Formula menu to display the Paste Name dialog box. The Paste Name list box shows all the range names in the active sheet.

```
┌─────────────────────────────────┐
│ ─           Paste Name           │
│ ┌─Paste Name──┐     ┌────────┐  │
│ │ Expenses    │▲    │   OK   │  │
│ │ Inflation   │     └────────┘  │
│ │ Margin      │     ┌────────┐  │
│ │ Revenue     │     │ Cancel │  │
│ │             │     └────────┘  │
│ │             │     ┌──────────┐│
│ │             │     │Paste List││
│ │             │▼    └──────────┘│
│ │             │     ┌────────┐  │
│ └─────────────┘     │  Help  │  │
│                     └────────┘  │
└─────────────────────────────────┘
```

3. Select the name you want to insert in the currently selected cell, and select OK to complete the process.

NOTES If the formula bar isn't active, Excel activates it and enters an equals sign (=) before pasting the name.

The Paste List button on the Paste Name dialog box allows you to paste a two column list of names and range definitions in a selected area of your worksheet. Move the selection cursor to the worksheet location where you want to paste the list, and then use the Paste Name command Paste List button to complete the operation.

NEW FILES

MENU PATH File ➤ New

SHORTCUTS Shift-F11, Alt-Shift-F1, New Worksheet tool (open new worksheets); F11, Alt-F1 (open new charts); Ctrl-F11, Alt-Ctrl-F1 (open new macro sheets)

The New command creates and opens a new worksheet, macro sheet, chart, workbook, or slides file. To use the New command, follow these steps:

1. Choose the New command from the File menu, or select the New Worksheet tool from the tool bar to display the New dialog box.

2. Choose a worksheet, chart, macro sheet, workbook, or slides from the list box, and select OK to display the new file.

NOTE When you create a new chart file, Excel uses the data in the selected range of the active worksheet to create a chart.

SEE ALSO Charting Features, Opening Files, Saving Files in a Workbook

NEW WINDOWS

MENU PATH Window ➤ New Window

The New Window command creates another document window in the active window. If you've constructed a large worksheet and want to view different parts of the worksheet at the same time, you can use the New Window command to create the additional windows.

SEE ALSO Splitting Windows into Panes

NOTES ON CELLS

MENU PATH Formula ➤ Note

SHORTCUT Shift-F2

The Note command lets you attach textual notes to cells so you can document or explain the contents of a cell. Cell notes can be edited and printed much like other Excel documents. Choose the Note command from the Formula menu to display the Cell Note dialog box.

To attach a note to a cell, enter the cell address in the Cell text box and then type the note in the Text Note box.

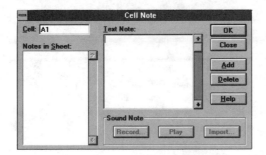

NOTES If you select a cell before selecting the Note command, Excel automatically enters the cell's address in the Cell Note dialog box.

To see your cell notes, choose the Note command, and select the cell from the Notes in Sheet list to display the note in the Text Note box.

Cells that have attached notes are marked with a small red square on the upper-right corner when displayed on a worksheet.

For more information on how to use the Sound Note command buttons, consult your Microsoft Excel User Guide.

OBJECT MOVEMENT TO BACK AND FRONT

MENU PATH Format ➤ Send to Back/Bring to Front

The Send to Back command moves the selected object in a worksheet to the bottom of a stack of objects. The Bring to Front command moves the selected object in a worksheet to the top of a stack of objects. Select the object you want to move, and choose the appropriate command.

SEE ALSO Drawing Features, Grouping Graphic Objects, Object Property Control

OBJECT PROPERTY CONTROL

MENU PATH Format ➤ Object Properties

The Object Properties Command lets you control how graphic objects are connected to worksheets and how these objects change when the cells they are connected to change. To use the command, follow these steps:

1. Select the object for which you want to change properties.

2. Choose the Object Properties command to display the Object Properties dialog box.

```
┌─ ─────────── Object Properties ───────────┐
│ ┌─Object Placement──────────┐  ┌────────┐ │
│ │ ⦿ Move and Size with Cells │  │   OK   │ │
│ │ ○ Move but Don't Size with Cells│ ┌──────┐│
│ │ ○ Don't Move or Size with Cells│ │Cancel││
│ └───────────────────────────┘  └──────┘  │
│ ⊠ Print Object              ┌──────┐      │
│                             │ Help │      │
│                             └──────┘      │
└───────────────────────────────────────────┘
```

3. Mark the appropriate option buttons to control the object's properties when it's associated cells are moved.

4. To print the object when the worksheet to which it's connected prints, mark the Print Object checkbox.

5. Select OK to complete the process.

SEE ALSO Drawing Features, Grouping Graphic Objects, Object Movement Back to Front

OPENING FILES

MENU PATH File ➤ Open

SHORTCUTS Ctrl-F12, Open file tool

The Open command lets you retrieve files saved on disk. To use the Open command, follow these steps:

1. Choose the Open command from the File menu or use the Open file tool on the tool bar to display the File Open dialog box.

2. Move the selection cursor to the Drives list box, and specify the disk that contains your file.

3. Move the selection cursor to the Directories list box, and specify the appropriate directory.

4. Enter the file's name in the text box or select the file from the File Name list box.

5. Select OK to complete the process.

NOTE To retrieve files you only want to read but not modify or save, mark the Read Only check box.

SEE ALSO New Files

OPTIMIZATION MODELING

MENU PATH Formula ➤ Solver

The Solver command lets you perform linear and nonlinear programming. Linear and nonlinear programming solve problems in which an optimization function is maximized or minimized, subject to certain specified constraints.

To comfortably use the Solver command and safely rely on its results, you should understand optimization problem solving. Refer to your Microsoft Excel User Guide for more information on the mechanics of the Solver command.

SEE ALSO Target Value Modeling, What-If Modeling

OUTLINING WORKSHEET DATA

MENU PATH Formula ➤ Outline

The Formula Outline command lets you compress your worksheet data in outline form. To outline your worksheet, first select the range you want outlined, choose the Outline command, and then select the Create button from the dialog box.

NOTE For more information on the Outline command, refer to your Microsoft Excel User Guide.

PAGE BREAKS

MENU PATH Options ➤ Set Page Break

The Set Page Break command lets you set page breaks for printing. To specify a horizontal page break, select the row above where the page break should occur. For a vertical page break, select the column to the left of where the page should break. When you've selected the appropriate row or column, choose the Set Page Break command from the Options menu.

NOTE If a page break has been set at the selected row or column, Excel displays the Remove Page Break command.

SEE ALSO Setting Print Areas, Setting Print Titles

PAGE SETUP

MENU PATH File ➤ Page Setup

The Page Setup command lets you specify appearance, orientation, and scaling for your printed pages from a wide variety of options. To use the Page Setup command, follow these steps:

1. Choose the Page Setup command from the File menu to display the Page Setup dialog box.

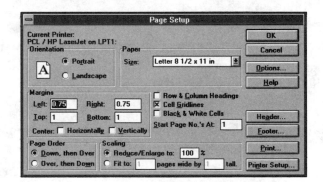

2. Enter, mark, and select the appropriate setup options on the dialog box, and then select OK to complete the process.

NOTES The Page Order option buttons break a worksheet into columns or rows so the worksheet prints down and then over by columns, or over and then down by rows.

To enlarge or reduce a document to fit on a certain number of pages, use the Fit To pages text boxes.

SEE ALSO Print Preview

PARSING IMPORTED TEXT

MENU PATH Data ➤ Parse

The Parse command lets you parse a long text label in a single cell into segments spread across several cells in a row. You can parse one row or several rows. The Parse command is often used when importing text from nonspreadsheet applications.

NOTE For more information, refer to your Microsoft Excel User Guide.

PASTING DATA FROM THE CLIPBOARD

MENU PATH Edit ➤ Paste

SHORTCUT Shift-Ins

The Paste command on the Edit and Shortcuts menus copies data currently stored in the Windows clipboard to selected locations on worksheets or charts. Use the Paste command after you have used the Cut or Copy commands to move or copy data to the Clipboard.

To use the Paste command, first select the worksheet or chart location where you want to paste the Clipboard data, and then choose the Paste command.

NOTE You can use the Windows clipboard to move data between two Windows applications such as from Excel to Word.

SEE ALSO Copying Data to the Clipboard, Cutting Selected Worksheet Data, Pasting Special Clipboard Data

PASTING FUNCTIONS IN FORMULAS

MENU PATH Formula ➤ Paste Function

SHORTCUT Shift-F3

The Paste Function command makes it easier to work with worksheet and macro sheet functions by allowing you to paste function names and arguments into formulas you're creating or editing. To use the Paste Function command, follow these steps:

1. Position the insertion point at the exact location where you want the function inserted.

2. Choose the Paste Function command from the Formula menu to display the Paste Function dialog box.

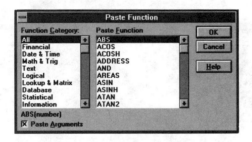

3. Select a category from the Function Category list, and then choose a function from the Paste Function list box.

NOTE To have Excel include one-word descriptions of a function's arguments, mark the Paste Arguments check box.

PASTING LINK FORMULAS

MENU PATH Edit ➤ Paste Link

The Edit menu's Paste Link command creates a link formula between two Excel documents. If you copy the contents of cell A1 in the worksheet named BUDGET.XLS and paste, using the Paste Link Command, those contents to cell

B2 in the worksheet named EXPENSES.XLS, Excel creates the link formula =BUDGET!A1 in cell B2 of EXPENSES.XLS.

SEE ALSO Copying Data to the Clipboard, Linking Files

PASTING SPECIAL CLIPBOARD DATA

MENU PATH Edit ➤ Paste Special

The Paste Special command copies only specified data from the Clipboard. Follow these steps, after using the Copy or Cut commands, to paste selected data from the Clipboard:

1. Choose the Edit menu's Paste Special command to display the Paste Special dialog box.

2. Use the option buttons to indicate the data you want to copy.

3. To skip pasting blanks from the Clipboard to the selected location on your worksheet, mark the Skip Blanks check box.

4. To transpose a range as it's pasted, making rows into columns or columns into rows, mark the Transpose check box.

5. To combine the values you're pasting from the Clipboard with the values in the destination range to perform an arithmetic operation, use the Operation buttons.

NOTES When you use the Paste Special command on data copied to the Clipboard by another application, Excel displays a modified version of the dialog box.

If you use the Paste Special command while working with charts, Excel displays a dialog box that asks how the data should be interpreted.

SEE ALSO Copying Data to the Clipboard, Cutting Selected Worksheet Data

PATTERNS AND CELL SHADING

MENU PATH Format ➤ Patterns

The Patterns command gives you control over how cells are shaded, including the colors used for shading foregrounds and backgrounds, and also the patterns used, such as diagonal lines, cross-hatching, and dots. To use the Patterns command, follow these steps:

1. Select the cell or worksheet range you want to shade.

2. Choose the Patterns command from the Format menu or the Shortcuts menu to display the Patterns dialog box.

```
┌─────────────────────────────────────────┐
│ ▬              Patterns                  │
├─────────────────────────────────────────┤
│ ┌─Cell Shading──────────┐  ┌────────┐    │
│ │ Pattern:  [None    ▼] │  │   OK   │    │
│ │                       │  └────────┘    │
│ │ Foreground:[Automatic▼]  ┌────────┐    │
│ │                       │  │ Cancel │    │
│ │ Background:[Automatic▼]  └────────┘    │
│ └───────────────────────┘  ┌────────┐    │
│                            │  Help  │    │
│                            └────────┘    │
│                            ┌─Sample──┐   │
│                            │         │   │
│                            │         │   │
│                            └─────────┘   │
└─────────────────────────────────────────┘
```

3. Activate the Pattern drop down list box and select the pattern you want to use for shading.

4. Activate the Foreground drop down list box and select the color you want to use for the shading pattern.

5. Activate the Background drop down list box and select the color you want to use as a background behind the shading pattern.

SEE ALSO Automatic Formatting, Bordering and Shading Cells and Ranges

PRINT PREVIEW

MENU PATH File ➤ Print Preview

The Print Preview command displays a window showing what each of your pages should look like printed.

P

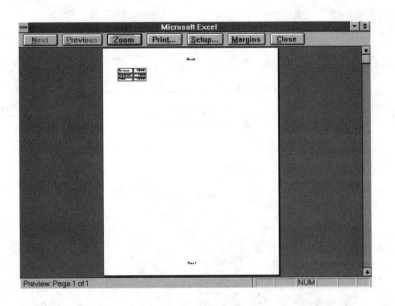

To view other pages in a document, use the Next and Previous buttons. To magnify a page, use the Zoom button. To print the document, use the Print button. You can also use the Setup and Margins command buttons to change the way the page is printed. To remove the Print Preview window from your display, select the Close command button.

SEE ALSO Page Setup, Printing

PRINT REPORT

MENU PATH File ➤ Print Report

The Print Report command displays the Print Report dialog box that allows you to print predefined reports. A predefined report is comprised of a view, or set of print settings, and a scenario created by the Formula menu's Scenario Manager command. You can also use the Print Report dialog box to create, edit, and delete predefined reports.

SEE ALSO Printing, What-If Modeling

PRINTING

MENU PATH File ➤ Print

SHORTCUTS Ctrl-Shift-F12, Print tool

The Print command prints the worksheet, chart, or macro sheet in the active window. To use the Print command, follow these steps:

1. Choose the Print command from the File menu or the Print tool from the tool bar to display the Print dialog box.

2. Use the Print Range options to designate the number of pages you want to print.

3. The Print Quality list box lets you select a print quality supported by your printer.

4. The Print option buttons let you print just a worksheet, the notes attached to the cells in a worksheet, or both.

5. Enter the number of copies you want to print.

6. To display your document in the Print Preview window before printing it, mark the Preview check box.

NOTE The Page Setup command button activates the Page Setup dialog box. The page setup features let you specify appearance, orientation, and scaling for your printed pages from a variety of options.

SEE ALSO Page Setup, Print Preview, Setting Print Areas, Setting Print Titles

PRODUCT SUPPORT

MENU PATH Help ➤ Product Support

The Product Support command starts the Windows Help application and shows the Microsoft Product Support available for Excel.

SEE ALSO Help on Excel

PROTECTING DOCUMENTS

MENU PATH Options ➤ Protect Document

The Protect Document command turns on cell-level, object-level, and window-level document protection. When you select the Protect Document command, Excel displays the Protect Document dialog box.

You can specify the type of document protection and a password for disabling document protection. With cell-level protection, cells marked as locked can't be modified and cells marked as hidden can't have their contents viewed on the formula bar. Object-level protection prevents objects embedded in documents from being modified. Window-level protection keeps windows from being modified.

NOTE The Unprotect Document command appears on the Options menu when document protection is enabled. If a password was entered when document protection was turned on, the Unprotect Document command displays a dialog box to collect the password.

SEE ALSO Cell Protection

Q+E APPLICATION

Q+E is a separate application that lets you work with databases. Using Q+E, you can access and update database files created by many popular database applications, including dBASE files, SQL Server files, Oracle files, and even Microsoft Excel files if they have a defined database.

NOTE For more information on the Q+E application, refer to your Q+E for Microsoft Excel User Guide.

REPEATING THE LAST COMMAND

MENU PATH Edit ➤ Repeat

SHORTCUT Alt-Enter

The Repeat command simply repeats the last command chosen. Excel continually updates the name of the Repeat command to reflect the last selected command.

NOTE If you just pasted something using the Edit menu's Paste command, the full name of the Repeat command would be Repeat Paste.

REPLACING CELL DATA

MENU PATH Formula ➤ Replace

The Replace command lets you search through worksheet and macro sheet cells for specific labels, values, formulas, or pieces of formulas, and then replace them. To use the Replace command, follow these steps:

1. Select the worksheet range you want to search.

2. Choose the Replace command from the Formula menu to display the Replace dialog box.

3. Enter the label, value, formula, or formula fragment you want to search for in the Find What text box.

4. Enter the label, value, formula, or formula fragment you want to substitute in the Replace With text box.

5. Use the Look At option buttons to tell Excel to exactly or partly match a cell's contents.

6. Use the Look By option buttons to tell Excel to search by rows or columns.

7. The Match Case check box tells Excel to search for only exact matches in case with the text in the Find What box.

8. Select the Replace All, Find Next, or Replace command buttons to initiate the search.

NOTE The Replace All button replaces all occurrences. The Find Next and Replace command buttons let you individually locate and replace occurrences. To terminate the Replace operation, select the Close command button.

ROW HEIGHT CHANGES

MENU PATH Format ➤ Row Height

The Row Height command lets you increase, decrease, or hide rows. To use the command, follow these steps:

1. Select the row or rows you want to change.

2. Choose the Row Height command from either the Format menu or the Shortcuts menu to display the Row Height dialog box.

3. Enter the desired row height in points in the Row Height text box, and then select OK to complete the process.

NOTES To reset row height to the default dimension (12.75 points) mark the Standard Height check box.

To hide a row, select the Hide command button. To unhide a row, select a range that includes the rows both above and below the hidden row, choose the Row Height command, and select the Unhide command button from the dialog box.

SAVING FILES

MENU PATH File ➤ Save/Save As

SHORTCUTS Shift+F12 (Save), F12 (Save As), Save File tool

The File menu's Save command saves files that have already been named and as-signed a disk storage location. If a file hasn't already been assigned a name and storage location and you choose the Save command or select the Save File tool, Excel executes the Save As command.

Use the Save As command to name and save files that haven't previously been saved. To use the Save As command, follow these steps:

1. Choose the Save As command from the File menu or select the Save file tool from the tool bar. Excel displays the File Save As dialog box.

2. Use the Drives list box to specify the disk where you want to store the file.
3. The Directories list box lets you specify the directory.
4. Use the File Name text box to enter a valid DOS file name. Excel adds a 3-letter extension for you.

NOTES To save files in formats other than Excel, activate the Save File As Type list box and select the appropriate file format.

If you select the Options command button on the File Save As dialog box, Excel lets you create Backup copies of files, add passwords, and create read-only files.

SEE ALSO Saving Files in a Workbook

SAVING FILES IN A WORKBOOK

MENU PATH File ➤ Save Workbook

The Save Workbook command lets you save worksheets, macros and charts in a single file called a workbook. If you later open a workbook, Excel opens each item in the workbook file. To use the Save Workbook command, follow these steps:

1. Choose the Save Workbook command from the File menu to display the File Save As dialog box.

2. Use the Drives, Directories, and File Name boxes to enter a valid DOS workbook file name and specify the disk and directory locations for your file. Excel adds an .XLW file extension for you.

NOTE When a workbook file is open, Excel lists a workbook contents window showing each file in the group. The workbook contents window can be used to add and remove files.

SEE ALSO New Files, Opening Files, Saving Files

SELECTING SPECIAL CELL CHARACTERISTICS

MENU PATH Formula ➤ Select Special

The Select Special command selects cells with certain specified characteristics. To use the command, follow these steps:

1. Select the worksheet range you want to search.

2. Choose the Select Special command from the Formula menu to display the Select Special dialog box.

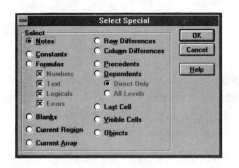

3. Mark the appropriate option buttons to locate:

- ◆ Cells with notes attached.

- ◆ Constants specified with the Numbers, Text, Logical Values, and Errors check boxes.

- ◆ Formulas that return results specified with the Numbers, Text, Logical Values, and Errors check boxes.

- ◆ Blanks or empty cells.

- ◆ The Current Region or the rectangle that surrounds the active cell.

- ◆ The Current Array that includes the active cell.

- ◆ The Row Differences of cells whose contents differ from those in the column to the left.

- ◆ The Column Differences of cells whose contents differ from those in the row above.

- ◆ The Precedents upon which formulas in the selected range depend specified with the Direct Only or All Levels buttons.

- ◆ The Dependents of cells with formulas in the selected range specified with the Direct Only or the All Levels buttons.

- ◆ The Last Cell at the intersection of the right most column and bottom most row to hold data or be formatted.

- ◆ The Visible Cells in the selected range.

- ◆ The Objects imbedded in the worksheet.

4. Select OK to complete the process.

SEE ALSO Finding Cell Data

SERIES VALUES

MENU PATH Data ➤ Series

The Series command enters a series of values into a selected range of a worksheet. You can use the Series command to enter values that increase or decrease arithmetically or exponentially. You can also use the Series command to enter date values that increase or decrease by units of time.

To use the command, enter the starting value for the series in one cell, and select the range including the starting value and each of the other cells you want filled. Choose the Series command from the Data menu to display the Series dialog box. Make your selections on the dialog box, and then select OK to complete the process.

SEE ALSO Filling Cell Data into Selected Ranges

SETTING CRITERIA FOR DATABASE SEARCH

MENU PATH Data ➤ Set Criteria

The Set Criteria command on the Data menu is used to identify the worksheet range where you entered the search criteria required for the Data menu's Find, Extract, and Delete commands. To use the command, enter your search criteria in a worksheet, select the range containing the criteria, and then choose the Set Criteria command.

NOTE For a tutorial on specifying database search criteria, refer to Lesson 7.

SEE ALSO Setting Database Ranges, Setting Extraction Ranges

SETTING DATABASE RANGES

MENU PATH Data ➤ Set Database

The Set Database command identifies the worksheet range where database field names and records are stored. To create a database with the Set Database command, enter your database records in a worksheet using the Data menu's Form command, select the range that contains your database records, and then choose the Set Database command from the Data menu.

NOTES The first row or column of a selected database range should contain the database field names, and the selected range must also include at least one other row or column even if that row or column is blank.

For detailed information on creating and working with databases, refer to Lesson 7.

SEE ALSO Form for Data Entry

SETTING EXTRACTION RANGES

MENU PATH Data ➤ Set Extract

The Set Extract command lets you identify the worksheet range where extracted records are pasted. To use the command, select the worksheet range where you want to paste the extracted records, and then choose the Set Extract command.

NOTES The first row of the extract range should contain the database field names of the record fields you want pasted.

For a tutorial on finding and extracting database records, refer to Lesson 7.

SEE ALSO Setting Criteria for Database Search, Setting Database Ranges

SETTING PRINT AREAS

MENU PATH Options ➤ Set Print Area

The Set Print Area command lets you specify one or more worksheet ranges for printing. To use the Set Print Area command, select the worksheet range or ranges you want to print, and then choose the Set Print Area command from the Options menu. Excel names the selected range *Print Area* and then prints that named range when you choose the Print command from the File menu or use the Print tool on the tool bar.

NOTE Unless you set a print area, Excel prints your entire worksheet when you use the Print command.

SEE ALSO Printing

SETTING PRINT TITLES

MENU PATH Options ➤ Set Print Titles

The Set Print Titles command lets you specify selected rows or columns to be printed as borders on each document page. To use the Set Print Titles command, follow these steps:

1. Choose the Set Print Titles command from the Options menu to display the Set Print Titles dialog box.

2. Enter the address of the rows or columns you want to use as borders in the appropriate text boxes.

3. Select OK to complete the process.

NOTE The column or row address you specify must be absolute. For example, to use rows 1 and 2 as a horizontal border, enter $1:$2.

SEE ALSO Page Breaks, Printing

SHOWING THE ACTIVE CELL

MENU PATH Formula ➤ Show Active Cell

The Show Active Cell command moves the sheet displayed in the active window so the active cell is visible. The active cell is the cell with the cell selector.

SORTING WORKSHEET DATA

MENU PATH Data ➤ Sort

The Data menu's Sort command lets you sort, or organize, any group of worksheet cells or database records. To use the Sort command, follow these steps:

1. Select the range holding the cells or database records you want to sort.

2. Choose the Sort command to display the Sort dialog box.

3. Mark the Rows or Columns option button to choose a method for sorting your selected range.

4. Select the 1st Key for sorting by entering the address, as an absolute reference, of the cell that contains the label, value, or database field you want to sort by.

5. Mark the Ascending or Descending option buttons to tell Excel how to sort your data.

6. Specify 2nd and 3rd Key settings to accomodate labels, values, or database fields that may be identical to previously selected keys.

SPELL-CHECKING DOCUMENTS

MENU PATH Options ➤ Spelling

The Spelling command checks the spelling of words on the formula bar or in a selected worksheet range. To use the Spelling command, follow these steps:

1. Select the cells whose labels and notes you want to check for misspelled words. If you want to check the spelling of words on the formula bar, select the words in the formula you want to check. Excel checks all the words in the active worksheet if you do not make a specific selection.

2. Choose the Spelling command from the Options menu.

3. When Excel finds a word not in its dictionary, it displays the word in the Spelling dialog box.

4. Type a replacement word in the Change To text box, select one of the suggested spellings from the Suggestions list, or use the Ignore command button if you're satisfied with the current spelling.

5. Select the Change button to change the identified word to a new spelling you've designated.

NOTE For a detailed tutorial on the Spelling command, refer to Lesson 2.

SPLITTING WINDOWS INTO PANES

MENU PATH Window ➤ Split

The Split command breaks windows into two or four pieces, called panes. Because one window pane can be scrolled independently of the others, the Split command makes it possible for you to view different portions of the same worksheet.

NOTES If the active document is split, the Window menu displays the Remove Split command.

The size of each pane can be adjusted. Consult your Microsoft Excel User Guide for more information.

SEE ALSO Freezing Panes on Split Document Windows

STYLES FOR WORKSHEET FORMATTING

MENU PATH Format ➤ Style

SHORTCUTS Style box tool, Paste formats tool

The Style command lets you define formatting styles. A formatting style is a set of formatting rules, including number, font, alignment, border, patterns, and cell protection formatting. To define a new formatting style, choose the Style command. Excel displays a dialog box that allows you to specify a set of formatting rules and name them as a style.

To use a named format style, select the worksheet range where you want the style applied, and then select the style from the Style box on the tool bar.

SEE ALSO Aligning Values and Labels, Automatic Formatting, Bordering and Shading Cells, Font Styles, Formatting Numbers, Justifying Text, Patterns and Cell Shading.

TABLE COMMAND SCENARIOS

MENU PATH Data ➤ Table

The Table command lets you quickly perform "what-if " analysis with one or two input values. To use the Table command, first build a worksheet model including the formula and the series of input values you want to recalculate. The Table command performs a what-if analysis that recalculates the formula for each of the input values.

NOTE For more information, refer to your Microsoft Excel User Guide.

SEE ALSO What-If Modeling

TARGET VALUE MODELING

MENU PATH Formula ➤ Goal Seek

The Goal Seek command lets you solve target value models to find the single input value that causes a dependent formula to return a desired target value. To use the Goal Seek command, follow these steps:

1. Build a worksheet model with the formula you want to return a specific target value in one cell, and the formula input that returns the target value in another cell.

2. Choose the Goal Seek command from the Formula menu to display the Goal Seek dialog box.

Goal Seek	
Set cell: B4	OK
To value: 1000000	Cancel
By changing cell: B2	Help

3. Enter the formula cell address in the Set cell text box.

4. Enter the target value in the To value text box.

5. Enter the input value cell address in the By changing cell text box.

6. Select the OK command button to initiate the target value calculations, and Excel displays the Goal Seek Status dialog box.

```
┌─────────────────────────────────────────┐
│ ▭        Goal Seek Status                │
├─────────────────────────────────────────┤
│ Goal Seeking with Cell B5      ┌───────┐ │
│ found a solution.              │  OK   │ │
│                                └───────┘ │
│ Target Value:  1000000         ┌───────┐ │
│ Current Value: 1000000         │Cancel │ │
│                                └───────┘ │
│                                ┌───────┐ │
│                                │ Step  │ │
│                                └───────┘ │
│                                ┌───────┐ │
│                                │ Pause │ │
│                                └───────┘ │
│                                ┌───────┐ │
│                                │ Help  │ │
│                                └───────┘ │
└─────────────────────────────────────────┘
```

7. Select one of the following command buttons to complete the process.

   ◆ OK closes the dialog box and places the value that causes the formula to return the target value in the input cell.

   ◆ Cancel closes the dialog box without changing the input cell value.

   ◆ Step incrementally steps through the target value calculations, one input value at a time.

   ◆ Pause temporarily suspends target value calculation. To restart calculations select the Continue button.

SEE ALSO Optimization Modeling, What-If Modeling

TOOL BAR CONTROL

MENU PATH Options ➤ Toolbars

The Toolbars command lets you control whether or not Excel displays a tool bar beneath the menu bar. It also lets you display different tool bars for outlining, charting, and so on. You can even create new tool bars and customize existing ones by adding and removing command buttons.

UNDOING MISTAKES

MENU PATH Edit ➤ Undo

SHORTCUTS Ctrl-Z, Alt-Backspace

The Undo command reverses the effect of most data entry and worksheet editing actions. To use the command, simply choose it from the Edit menu after you've done something you wish you hadn't.

NOTE After choosing the Undo command, Excel displays the Redo command so you can redo what you just undid.

UNHIDING DOCUMENT WINDOWS

MENU PATH Window ➤ Unhide

The Unhide command displays a dialog box listing hidden windows. To unhide a previously hidden window, simply select it from the list.

SEE ALSO Hiding Document Windows

U

VIEWING DOCUMENT WINDOW FORMATS

MENU PATH Window ➤ View

The View command lets you create different views of a window. A view includes things like print settings, row and column widths, display settings, and even window size.

NOTE For more information on the View command, refer to your Microsoft Excel User Guide.

V

WHAT-IF MODELING

MENU PATH Formula ➤ Scenario Manager

The Scenario Manager command performs what-if analysis that lets you experiment with changing formula results as one or more inputs change. To use the scenario manager, follow these steps:

1. Build a worksheet model including the output value formula in one cell, and the variable input value in another cell.

2. Choose the Scenario Manager command from the Formula menu to display the Scenario Manager dialog box.

```
┌─────────────────────────────────┐
│ ▬        Scenario Manager        │
├─────────────────────────────────┤
│ Scenarios:              ┌──────┐ │
│ No scenarios defined.   │ Show │ │
│ Specify all the         └──────┘ │
│ Changing Cells, then    ┌──────┐ │
│ choose "Add..." to      │ Close│ │
│ add scenarios.          └──────┘ │
│                         ┌──────┐ │
│                         │ Add..│ │
│                         └──────┘ │
│                         ┌──────┐ │
│                         │Delete│ │
│                         └──────┘ │
│                         ┌──────┐ │
│                         │ Edit │ │
│ Changing Cells:         └──────┘ │
│ ┌─────────────────────┐ ┌──────┐ │
│ │$A$1                 │ │Summary│ │
│ └─────────────────────┘ └──────┘ │
│ Ctrl+Click cells to select ┌────┐│
│ non-adjacent cells         │Help││
│                            └────┘│
└─────────────────────────────────┘
```

3. Enter the variable input value cell address in the Changing Cells text box.

4. To add input value scenarios, choose the Add button, and Excel displays the Add Scenario dialog box.

```
┌─────────────────────────────────┐
│ ▬           Add Scenario         │
├─────────────────────────────────┤
│ Name: ┌──────────────┐  ┌──────┐ │
│       │              │  │  OK  │ │
│       └──────────────┘  └──────┘ │
│ 1:  $A$1  ┌─────┐       ┌──────┐ │
│           │  0  │       │Cancel│ │
│           └─────┘       └──────┘ │
│                         ┌──────┐ │
│                         │ Add  │ │
│                         └──────┘ │
│                         ┌──────┐ │
│                         │ Help │ │
│                         └──────┘ │
└─────────────────────────────────┘
```

5. Enter a name for the scenario in the Name text box.

6. Enter the input value for the first scenario in the other text box, and select OK to return to the Scenario Manager dialog box.

7. To initiate a scenario, select it from the Scenarios list box, and then select the Show command button.

8. To create a scenario summary worksheet, select the Summary command button to display the Scenario Summary dialog box.

Scenario Summary

Changing Cells:
B2

Result Cells (optional):

OK
Cancel
Help

9. Enter the cell address of the output formula in the Result Cells text box. To test more than one output formula, enter each cell address in the text box, separating them with commas.

10. To create a summary worksheet, select OK.

NOTE To delete or edit a scenario, choose the Scenario Manager command and select the scenario from the list. To delete the scenario, select Delete. To edit the scenario by changing either the name or the input value, select Edit, and then make the needed changes using the Edit Scenario dialog box.

SEE ALSO Target Value Modeling, Table Command Scenarios

WORKSPACE SETTINGS

MENU PATH Options ➤ Workspace

The Workspace command controls how the Excel application window appears during an Excel session. You can designate how rows and columns are identified; whether the status bar, scroll bars, and formula bars appear; how the Info window looks, and if cell notes are flagged.

The Workspace command also gives you the ability to change several of the mechanical aspects of Excel. You can tell Excel to automatically enter decimal points, change the way the menu bar is activated, and specify an alternate set of navigation keys.

NOTE For more information on the Workspace command, refer to your Microsoft Excel User Guide.

ZOOMING IN OR OUT OF WINDOWS

MENU PATH Window ➤ Zoom

The Zoom command lets you magnify or reduce the size of the document displayed in the active window. When you select this command, Excel displays the Zoom dialog box.

To change the size of a document, select a Magnification option button. If you select the Custom button, enter the desired percentage in the text box.

INSTALLATION INSTRUCTIONS

Installing Excel 4.0 for Windows isn't difficult. If you haven't already installed the program, use the following step-by-step instructions.

1. Start Windows and display the Windows Program Manager.

2. Insert Excel Disk 1 into drive A.

3. Choose the Run command from the File menu to display the Run dialog box.

4. Type **A:Setup** in the Command Line text box.

5. Press ↵ twice to bypass the two introductory message boxes.

6. Select the type of installation you want from the next message box.

7. By default, your Excel program and data files are installed in C:\EXCEL. When the next message box appears, press ↵ or enter the path for another directory in the text box provided.

If the directory where you want Excel installed doesn't already exist, Excel asks if you want it created. Select Yes, and Excel creates the required directory for you.

8. The next message box asks if you want to enable help for Lotus 1-2-3 users and use Excel with Lotus command styles. Press ↵ to accept the default setting or select Yes to use the Lotus 1-2-3 features.

9. Insert other setup disks as Excel prompts you, and press ↵ to continue.

As Excel copies files to your hard disk, it displays a message box that shows you the progress of the setup operation. When setup is complete, the Microsoft Excel 4.0 program group is added to your Windows Program Manager.

When you first start Excel, it displays an introduction screen with command buttons for selecting tutorials on Excel basics, the new features for Excel 4.0, and converting from Lotus 1-2-3. To skip these tutorials, select the Exit button.

INDEX

active printers, 37
add-in macro files, 69
addresses, cell, 5
aligning labels and values, 8, 27–28, 69–70
analysis tools, 70–71
application window, 5
applying range names, 109–110
automatic formatting, 26, 71–72
automatic keystrokes. *See* macros
AVERAGE function, 9
axes for charts, 49

Backspace key, 7
Bold style, 30–31, 89
borders, 31–32, 73

cell addresses, 5
cells, 5
    active, 5, 136
    characteristics of, 132–133
    erasing, 20, 76
    inserting, 19
    notes on, 113–114
    protecting, 75–76, 126
    references to, 18, 40, 56–57, 106–107
    shading, 31, 73, 123
    sorting, 33, 137
cell selector, 5–6, 15, 93
characteristics of cells, 132–133
charts, 45
    with Chart tool bar, 50–51
    with ChartWizard tool, 46–49, 76
    printing, 52
    saving, 51–52
Chart tool bar, 50–51
ChartWizard tool, 46–49, 76
circular references, 9
clearing data, 16–17, 76
clipboard, 79–80, 120, 122
closing files, 41, 77
colons (:), 9
colors
    for fonts, 31, 89
    for help, 96
    for printing, 37
    for shading, 31, 73, 123
    for windows, 77–78

columns, 5
    deleting, 20, 81
    hiding, 33, 78–79
    inserting, 19, 99
    in printing, 37, 40–41, 136
    width of, 32–33, 78–79
commands
    with macros, 56
    repeating, 129
comparisons in database queries, 64
consolidating data, 79
copying data and formulas, 17–18, 79
correcting mistakes, 7, 15, 143
criteria in database searches, 63–65, 134
CUSTOM.DIC file, 22
cutting data, 17–18, 80

databases, 59
    creating, 60–61
    defining, 60
    deleting records from, 81
    editing, 62
    extracting records from, 65, 85, 135
    finding records in, 63–65, 88, 134
    printing, 65–66
    Q+E application for, 62, 127
    ranges for, 134–135
    retrieving, 65–66
    saving, 65–66
    sorting, 62–63
data points, 46
Delete key, 7
deleting
    cells, 20
    columns, 20, 81
    database records, 81
    files, 42, 82
    rows, 20, 81
    scenarios, 148
demonstrations, 100
dictionaries, spelling, 22, 138
directories
    for Excel, 152
    for worksheets, 10, 14
displaying windows, 82–83
documents, protecting, 126
document windows, 5. *See also* windows

dollar signs ($), 18, 40
drawing, 83
drives for worksheets, 10, 14

editing, 13
    cells, 19–20
    columns, 19–20
    databases, 62
    with find, 20–21, 87–88
    ranges, 15–19
    and recalculations, 14–15, 75
    with replace, 21, 129–130
    rows, 19–20
    scenarios, 148
    and spell checking, 21–22, 137–138

entering
    database records, 60–61
    forms for, 90
    formulas, 8–9
    labels, 7
    values, 8
equal signs (=), 8–9
erasing
    cells, 76
    ranges, 16–17
exiting, 10, 85
exporting files, 43
extracting database records, 65, 85, 135

fields, 60–61
files
    add-in macro, 69
    for charts, 51–52
    closing, 41, 77
    creating, 112
    deleting, 42, 82
    exporting, 43–44
    importing, 43–44
    linking, 103
    for macros, 57, 69
    multiple, 41–42
    opening, 14, 41–42, 57, 112, 116
    saving, 10, 131–132
filling ranges, 18–19, 87
finding
    cell data, 20–21, 87–88
    database records, 63–65, 88, 134
    help topics, 96
fonts, 30–31, 89
formats for exporting and importing data, 43
formatting, 25
    alignment for, 27–28
    automatic, 26, 71–72
    borders and shading for, 31–32, 73
    charts, 50
    columns, 32–33
    erasing, 17
    fonts for, 30–31, 89
    rows, 32–33

    styles for, 29, 139
    values, 28–29, 90–91
forms for data entry, 90
formula bar, 5, 7
formulas
    copying, 18
    entering, 8–9
    erasing, 17
    for linking files, 103, 121–122
    pasting, 121–122
freezing panes, 91
functions, 9, 121

GLOBAL.XLM file, 54, 57, 106
goal seeking, 141–142
Goto command, 6, 93
graphic objects
    grouping, 93–94
    inserting, 99–100
    macros assigned to, 107
    position of, 115
    properties of, 115–116
    protecting, 126
grids
    for charts, 50
    printing, 37
grouping
    objects, 93–94
    worksheets and macro sheets, 94

handles for selected ranges, 19
height of rows, 28, 32–33, 130
help, 6, 95–97
hiding
    cells, 76
    columns, 33, 78–79
    macros, 57
    rows, 130
    windows, 97, 143

imported text, parsing, 120
importing files, 43–44
inserting
    cells, 19
    columns, 19, 99
    objects, 99–100
    rows, 19, 99
installation, 152
introducing Excel, 100
Italic style, 30–31, 89

justifying labels, 28, 101

keystrokes, automatic. *See* macros

labels
    aligning, 27–28, 69–70
    entering, 7
    justifying, 28, 101
landscape orientation, 36
learning Excel, tutorial for, 103

legends for charts, 49
linear programming, 117
linking files, 103, 121–122
Lotus 1-2-3, help for users of, 95

macros, 53
    add-in files for, 69
    objects for, 107
    recording and running, 54–57, 105–106
    sheets for, 54, 57, 94
    tips for, 56–57
margins for printing, 36–39, 124
menu bar, 5
mistakes, correcting, 7, 15, 143
modeling
    optimization, 117
    target value, 141–142
    what-if, 147–148
moving
    charts, 49
    objects, 115
    windows, 71
    within worksheets, 5–6, 93
Multiplan, help for, 95
multiple files, 41–42

names
    of fields, 60
    of files, 10, 131
    of macros, 54, 105
    of ranges, 6, 15, 109–112
navigation keys, 6, 15
negative numbers, 8
nonlinear programming, 117
notes, 17, 113–114
numbers
    aligning, 27–28, 69–70
    entering, 8
    formatting, 28–29, 90–91

objects
    grouping, 93–94
    inserting, 99–100
    macros assigned to, 107
    position of, 115
    properties of, 115–116
    protecting, 126
opening files, 14, 41–42, 57, 112, 116
operators, 9, 64
optimization modeling, 117
orientation, printing, 36
outlines, 117

page breaks, 41, 119
page setup, 36–37, 119–120
panes, 91, 138
paper size, 36
parentheses (), 9
parsing imported text, 120
passwords, 126

pasting
    cell data, 17–18, 120, 122
    functions, 121
    link formulas, 121–122
    range names, 111–112
patterns, 123
pausing macro recording, 57, 106
points, 30–31, 89
portrait orientation, 36
position
    of objects, 115
    of windows, 71
precedence of operators, 9
previewing printing, 38–39, 123–124
print areas, setting, 39–40, 135–136
printing, 35, 125
    charts, 52
    databases, 65
    fonts for, 31
    macro sheets, 57
    options for, 39–41
    page setup for, 36–37, 119–120
    previewing, 38–39, 123–124
    records, 65–66
    reports, 124
    scaling, 37
    scenarios, 124
    titles, 40–41, 136
product demonstrations, 100
product support, 126
properties of objects, 115–116
protecting cells and documents, 75–76, 126

Q+E application, 62, 127
querying database records, 63–65, 88, 134

ranges, 15
    aligning, 27–28
    for charts, 46
    copying, 17–18
    cutting, 17–18
    for databases, 134–135
    erasing, 16–17
    filling, 18–19, 87
    names for, 6, 15, 109–112
    pasting, 17–18
    printing, 39–40, 125
    protecting, 75–76
    series for, 134
recalculations, 14–15, 75
recording macros, 54–57, 105–106
records
    deleting, 81
    editing, 62
    entering, 60–61
    extracting, 65, 85, 135
    finding, 63–65, 88, 134
    printing, 65–66
    retrieving, 65–66

saving, 65–66
    sorting, 62–63
references, cell, 18, 40, 56–57, 106–107
repeating commands, 129
replacing data, 21, 129–130
reports, printing, 124
resuming macro recording, 106–107
retrieving
    databases, 66
    records, 65–66
    worksheets, 14
rows, 5
    deleting, 20, 81
    height of, 28, 32–33, 130
    inserting, 19, 99
    in printing, 37, 40–41, 136
running macros, 55–56, 105–106

saving
    charts, 51–52
    databases, 65
    files, 10, 131–132
    macro sheets, 57
    records, 65–66
    worksheets, 10, 131–132
scaling in printing, 37
scenarios
    printing, 124
    what-if analyses for, 147–148
scientific notation, 8
scroll bars, 5
searching
    for cell data, 20–21, 87–88, 129–130
    database records, 63–65, 88, 134
    for help topics, 96
series
    for charts, 46, 48
    for ranges, 134
shading, 31, 73, 123
SHEET1.XLS file, 41
shortcut keys, 16–17, 54–55, 105
single-stepping through macros, 55, 106
size
    of charts, 49
    of columns, 32–33, 78–79
    of fonts, 30–31, 89
    of paper, 36
    of rows, 28, 32–33, 130
    of windows, 71
Solver, 117
sorting
    cells, 33, 137
    databases, 62–63
spelling checker, 21–22, 137–138
split windows, 91, 138
starting Excel, 4
status bar, 5
stepping through macros, 55, 106
Strikeout style, 30–31, 89

styles
    of fonts, 30–31, 89
    for formatting, 29, 139
SUM function, 9
support, 126
.SYLK files, 43

tables for what-if analyses, 141
target value modeling, 141–142
text
    on charts, 50
    justifying, 101
    parsing, 120
title bar, 5
titles
    for charts, 49
    printing, 40–41, 136
tool bar, 5, 142
tutorials, 103, 152

Underline style, 30–31, 89
undoing mistakes, 15, 143
unhiding windows, 143

values
    aligning, 27–28, 69–70
    entering, 8
    formatting, 28–29, 90–91
    target, 141–142
viewing windows, 145

what-if analyses, 141, 147–148
width of columns, 32–33, 78–79
windows
    activating, 41
    application and document, 5
    colors for, 77–78
    creating, 113
    displaying, 82–83
    hiding, 97, 143
    position of, 71
    protecting, 126
    removing, 41
    size of, 71
    split, 91, 138
    viewing, 145
    zooming, 149
workbooks, saving files in, 132
worksheets
    creating, 7–9
    grouping, 94
    moving within, 5–6, 93
    outlines for, 117
    recalculating, 14–15, 75
    retrieving, 14
    saving, 10, 131–132
workspace settings, 148

zooming, 38–39, 124, 149

SYBEX

FREE BROCHURE!

Complete this form today, and we'll send you a full-color brochure of Sybex bestsellers.

Please supply the name of the Sybex book purchased.

_____

How would you rate it?

_____ Excellent   _____ Very Good   _____ Average   _____ Poor

Why did you select this particular book?

_____ Recommended to me by a friend

_____ Recommended to me by store personnel

_____ Saw an advertisement in _____

_____ Author's reputation

_____ Saw in Sybex catalog

_____ Required textbook

_____ Sybex reputation

_____ Read book review in _____

_____ In-store display

_____ Other _____

Where did you buy it?

_____ Bookstore

_____ Computer Store or Software Store

_____ Catalog (name: _____)

_____ Direct from Sybex

_____ Other: _____

Did you buy this book with your personal funds?

_____ Yes   _____ No

About how many computer books do you buy each year?

_____ 1-3   _____ 3-5   _____ 5-7   _____ 7-9   _____ 10+

About how many Sybex books do you own?

_____ 1-3   _____ 3-5   _____ 5-7   _____ 7-9   _____ 10+

Please indicate your level of experience with the software covered in this book:

_____ Beginner   _____ Intermediate   _____ Advanced

Which types of software packages do you use regularly?

_____ Accounting	_____ Databases	_____ Networks
_____ Amiga	_____ Desktop Publishing	_____ Operating Systems
_____ Apple/Mac	_____ File Utilities	_____ Spreadsheets
_____ CAD	_____ Money Management	_____ Word Processing
_____ Communications	_____ Languages	_____ Other _____

(please specify)

Which of the following best describes your job title?

_____ Administrative/Secretarial   _____ President/CEO

_____ Director   _____ Manager/Supervisor

_____ Engineer/Technician   _____ Other _____
                                                      (please specify)

Comments on the weaknesses/strengths of this book: _____

_____

_____

_____

_____

Name _____

Street _____

City/State/Zip _____

Phone _____

PLEASE FOLD, SEAL, AND MAIL TO SYBEX

SYBEX, INC.
Department M
2021 CHALLENGER DR.
ALAMEDA, CALIFORNIA USA
94501

SYBEX

SEAL

File
New...
Open...	Ctrl+F12
Close	
Links...	

Save	Shift+F12
Save As...	F12
Save Workbook...	
Delete...	

Print Preview
Page Setup...
Print...	Ctrl+Shift+F12
Print Report...	

Exit	Alt+F4

Edit
Undo Clear Ctrl+Z
Repeat Clear

Cut	Ctrl+X
Copy	Ctrl+C
Paste	Ctrl+V
Clear...	Del
Paste Special...	
Paste Link	

Delete...
Insert...
Insert Object...

Fill Right	Ctrl+R
Fill Down	Ctrl+D

Formula
Paste Function...

Define Name...
Create Names...
Apply Names...

Note...

Goto...	F5
Find...	Shift+F5
Replace...	
Select Special...	
Show Active Cell	

Outline...
Goal Seek...
Solver...
Scenario Manager...

Format
Number...

Alignment...
Font...
Border...
Patterns...
Cell Protection...

Style...
AutoFormat...

Row Height...
Column Width...

Justify

Bring to Front
Send to Back
Group
Object Properties...

Data
Form...

Find
Extract...
Delete
Set Database
Set Criteria
Set Extract

Sort...

Series...
Table...
Parse...
Consolidate...
Crosstab...

Options
Set Print Area

Set Print Titles...
Set Page Break

Display...
Toolbars...
Color Palette...

Protect Document...

Add-ins...
Calculation...
Workspace...

Spelling...

Group Edit...
Analysis Tools...

Macro
Run...

Record...

Start Recorder
Set Recorder
Relative Record
Assign to Object...
Resume

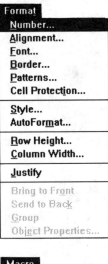

Window
New Window

Arrange...
Hide
Unhide...
View...

Split
Freeze Panes
Zoom...

√1 Sheet1

Help
Contents	F1

Search...
Product Support

Introducing Microsoft Excel
Learning Microsoft Excel

Lotus 1-2-3...
Multiplan Help...

About Microsoft Excel...